Pablo Coto-Millán

General Equilibrium and Welfare

With 45 Figures and 42 Tables

Physica-Verlag

A Springer-Verlag Company

Series Editors
Werner A. Müller
Martina Bihn

Author
Professor Pablo Coto-Millán
University of Cantabria
Department of Economics
Avda. de los Castros s/n.
39005 Santander
Spain

ISSN 1431-1933
ISBN 3-7908-1491-1 Physica-Verlag Heidelberg New York

Cataloging-in-Publication Data applied for
Die Deutsche Bibliothek – CIP-Einheitsaufnahme
Coto-Millán, Pablo: General equilibrium and welfare: with 42 tables / Pablo Coto-Millán. –
Heidelberg; New York: Physica-Verl., 2002
  (Contributions to economics)
  ISBN 3-7908-1491-1

Physica-Verlag Heidelberg New York
a member of BertelsmannSpringer Science+Business Media GmbH

© Physica-Verlag Heidelberg 2002
Printed in Germany

Softcover Design: Erich Kirchner, Heidelberg

SPIN 10875693   88/2202-5 4 3 2 1 0 – Printed on acid-free and non-aging paper

General Equilibrium and Welfare

Contributions to Economics

http://www.springer.de/cgi-bin/search_book.pl?series=1262

Peter Michaelis/Frank Stähler (Eds.)
**Recent Policy Issues in Environ-
mental and Resource Economics**
1998. ISBN 3-7908-1137-8

Jessica de Wolff
**The Political Economy
of Fiscal Decisions**
1998. ISBN 3-7908-1130-0

Georg Bol/Gholamreza Nakhaeizadeh/
Karl-Heinz Vollmer (Eds.)
**Risk Measurements, Econometrics
and Neural Networks**
1998. ISBN 3-7908-1152-1

Joachim Winter
**Investment and Exit Decisions
at the Plant Level**
1998. ISBN 3-7908-1154-8

Bernd Meyer
Intertemporal Asset Pricing
1999. ISBN 3-7908-1159-9

Uwe Walz
Dynamics of Regional Integration
1999. ISBN 3-7908-1185-8

Michael Carlberg
European Monetary Union
1999. ISBN 3-7908-1191-2

Giovanni Galizzi/
Luciano Venturini (Eds.)
**Vertical Relationships and
Coordination in the Food System**
1999. ISBN 3-7908-1192-0

Gustav A. Horn/Wolfgang Scheremet/
Rudolf Zwiener
Wages and the Euro
1999. ISBN 3-7908-1199-8

Dirk Willer
**The Development of Equity Capital
Markets in Transition Economies**
1999. ISBN 3-7908-1198-X

Karl Matthias Weber
**Innovation Diffusion and Political
Control of Energy Technologies**
1999. ISBN 3-7908-1205-6

Heike Link et al.
**The Costs of Road Infrastructure
and Congestion in Europe**
1999. ISBN 3-7908-1201-3

Simon Duindam
Military Conscription
1999. ISBN 3-7908-1203-X

Bruno Jeitziner
**Political Economy of the
Swiss National Bank**
1999. ISBN 3-7908-1209-9

Irene Ring et al. (Eds.)
Regional Sustainability
1999. ISBN 3-7908-1233-1

Katharina Müller/Andreas Ryll/
Hans-Jürgen Wagener (Eds.)
**Transformation of Social Security:
Pensions in Central-Eastern Europe**
1999. ISBN 3-7908-1210-2

Stefan Traub
Framing Effects in Taxation
1999. ISBN 3-7908-1240-4

Pablo Coto-Millán
Utility and Production
1999. ISBN 3-7908-1153-X

Frank Riedel
**Imperfect Information
and Investor Heterogeneity
in the Bond Market**
2000. ISBN 3-7908-1247-1

Kirsten Ralf
Business Cycles
2000. ISBN 3-7908-1245-5

Michele Bagella/
Leonardo Becchetti (Eds.)
**The Competitive Advantage
of Industrial Districts**
2000. ISBN 3-7908-1254-4

Frank Bohn
**Monetary Union and
Fiscal Stability**
2000. ISBN 3-7908-1266-8

Jaime Behar
**Cooperation and Competition in a
Common Market**
2000. ISBN 3-7908-1280-3

Michael Malakellis
**Integrated Macro-Micro-Modelling
Under Rational Expectations**
2000. ISBN 3-7908-1274-9

continued on page 177

Contents

Introduction

The GE theory uses a methodological approach characteristic of a closed and interrelated system where all the variables are simultaneously determined. This approach differs substantially from the partial equilibrium approach, where only some variables are relevant and the other ones are regarded as constant.

On the other hand, GE theory is a substantive or nuclear theory where the agents accept prices, transaction costs are null and markets include all goods and services for all temporal horizons. The requirements of this theory are relatively simple: a set preferences of the individuals, a set of production possibilities and an initial assignment of goods and inputs.

The three positive or non-standard results of this theory are: GE existence, unicity and stability. In order to demonstrate these results we proceed as follows: Starting from the model of an exchange economy (without production) we postulate a set of preferences and initial assignments in the model. The basic results of said model are the following:

i)   Existence of a GE without many graphic complexities.

ii)   The GE is a Pareto optimum (PO).

iii)   Another GE can be attained with the government's participation, in fact, any PO can be attained.

The truth is that there are anomalous cases, for example, the case of a corner equilibrium or Arrow's special case, where the PO is not a GE.

Does this GE have any desirable property? Yes, it does as this GE is a PO.

Moreover, this GE enables us to formulate the two Fundamental Welfare Economics Theorems.

The First Fundamental Welfare Economics Theorem: All GE is a Pareto-efficient allocation, in other words, it is a better than or at least as good an allocation as the remaining ones. On the other hand, GE satisfies the anonymity condition, that is to say, markets function with anonymous agents.

The Second Fundamental Welfare Economics Theorem: All GE previously chosen can be attained with a decentralized or competitive price mechanism.

The first theorem provides a desirable property to the GE model: efficiency.

The second theorem is highly appealing but it has scarce operative content due to the following three shortcomings:

i)   Prices must be taken as data. If the agents are of a specific size, for instance, a monopolist agent or various oligopolists, the prices of the goods and services could be decided by such agents.

ii)   The agents can be identified so anonymity is lost and it becomes very difficult to manage *lumpsum tax* transferences.

iii)   Although the public sector had all the information to implement *lumpsum tax* transferences the system should be inevitable.

Does GE deal with income distribution and equity?. Unfortunately, it doesn't.

When we first assess GE we find that not all the desirable properties are satisfied. Besides, many of the assumptions required for GE such as continuity and divisibility, non-convexity and gross substitutability are not very realistic. This leads to a negative prescriptive reading of GE. It is common that the economy presents multiplicity of equilibriums and also instabilities.

The first deficiency is that it is very difficult for GE to be stable and there is little likelihood that it has unicity properties. Is this really serious? Probably not. Take into account that demonstrations are sufficient (not necessary) and other properties may be discovered with time. At present there exists the hope - although not very much – of finding such new properties.

The second deficiency is relative to the quality of the model. Is the GE model a good model or isn't it? In order to answer this question we have two options. The first option consists of making a very plain model with few hypotheses, more or less an indispensable skeleton. In line with this, if we are very concise the theory is little determined and therefore, it is expected that more than one equilibrium and instability occurs.

The second option consists of making a very deterministic model with many hypotheses, like a perfectly dressed dummy. In this way, by being very deterministic, it will be difficult to represent a competitive economy in a stylized manner. However, in this case it more likely that one single equilibrium and stability exists.

As we face two extreme options, we may consider the search for a reasonable mid-point. To reach this point it could be enough to be capable of guaranteeing certain reasonable environmental conditions for consumers and producers. In other words, by avoiding pathological behaviors of the agents and preventing the income effects from being significant, we can guarantee unicity and stability.

The third deficiency refers to the assumptions. The basic assumptions supporting the model are very solid. In fact, the so-called market failures arise: problems in the allocation of property rights, information problems and choice and negotiation problems. The list of market failures could be more extensive, however, for the purposes here required, these three groups of problems are sufficient.

In addition to the three deficiencies or weaknesses above, the GE model does not include uncertainties, money or financial assets and its temporal reading is very mechanic. Uncertainty is an important issue for the financial world and aggregate policies. We must recognize how the degree of uncertainty affects the structure of the individual's preferences in such a way that the choices within a risk context become more complex. The GE model does not include full markets but, as we have mentioned, it has a very mechanic temporal reading: an umbrella is a different good today as compared with tomorrow and it has an infinite temporal horizon. If there are markets for all goods, one has to assume that there are futures markets for all commodities and products, which is not always possible. As a rule, markets are usually incomplete. Money and financial assets are not taken into account in the GE model since transaction costs are zero. In order to include money in the GE model, the following minimum requirements must be given:

i)   Money must have a positive price in all time periods.

ii)   The economy must be designed as an inter-temporal exchange process; successive generations' economies, for example.

iii)   Diverse or alternative financial assets must exist with uncertainty with respect to future. Moreover, the prices of these financial assets must be prevented from being so low that they can only go up.

In chapter 1 we do not intend to cover fully the theory of Competitive General Equilibrium (GE) but our aim is to present the most interesting ideas of that theory as well as demonstrating the existence, unicity and stability of GE. With this purpose, we offer demonstrations of fixed point, revealed preference as well as of local and global stability.

In chapter 2 we offer two models where multiple equilibriums and instabilities arise as a result from introducing very simple temporal dynamics. With these two models we want to illustrate the enormous sensitiveness of GE to the introduction of dynamic items in the models.

In chapter 3 we offer examples for distinct functional forms of equilibrium models. We have made an attempt to make illustrations with the simplest and most widely known functional forms such as the Cobb-Douglas.

In chapter 4 we offer a computable GE model: the Leontief model. Undoubtedly, there are more sophisticated computable versions of GE but the purpose of this chapter is to offer a plain computable GE model which enables us to know its use with some practical application.

Chapter 5 is dedicated to welfare. In it we present the GE problems classified into the above-mentioned three big groups of market failures.

To conclude with, in chapter 6 we present a thematic guide of issues concerning Social Choice.

1 General Equilibrium

1.1
Formal Interpretations of General Equilibrium (GE)

In this section we will show the two simplest models of GE: the pure exchange model and the GE model with production.

1.1.1 GE Model in Pure Exchange (Robinson Crusoe and Viernes): 2 Consumers

Assuming an economy made up by only 2 agents, A and B, which have an initial assignment of goods (x, y), these initial goods are like the "godsend". We are dealing with a non-production economy in which individuals can exchange their amounts of goods with the aim of maximizing satisfaction. Thus, we assume that each individual has a utility function of the type:

$$U_i(x_i, y_i); \text{ con } i = A, B$$

We also assume that the total amount available of the goods x and y will be the addition of the initial assignment of goods for each individual:

$$\overline{x}_A + \overline{x}_B = \overline{x}$$

$$\overline{y}_A + \overline{y}_B = \overline{y}$$

If each individual wants to maximize his utility function the problem for individual A can be presented as follows:

$$\max U_A(x_A, y_A)$$

$$\text{s. to} \quad \overline{x}_A + \overline{x}_B = \overline{x}$$

$$\overline{y}_A + \overline{y}_B = \overline{y}$$

$$U_B(x_B, y_B) = \overline{U}_B$$

For individual B the problem will be presented such as:

max $U_B(x_B, y_B)$

s. to $\overline{x}_A + \overline{x}_B = \overline{x}$

$\overline{y}_A + \overline{y}_B = \overline{y}$

$U_A(x_A, y_A) = \overline{U}_A$

In other words, each individual tries to maximize his utility considering the other individual's utility as fixed for a total amount of supply of each good equal to the amount which exists of each good.

The Lagrangian of the problem of individual A is:

$$L_A = U_A(x_A, y_A) - \lambda[U_B(x_B, y_B) - \overline{U}_B]$$

$$-\mu_1(\overline{x}_A + \overline{x}_B - \overline{x}) - \mu_2(\overline{y}_A + \overline{y}_B - \overline{y})$$

where λ is the multiplier of the restriction of utilities and ($\mu_1 y \ \mu_2$) are the multipliers of the restriction of resources.

The Lagrangian of the problem for individual B is:

$$L_B = U_B(x_B, y_B) - \gamma[U_A(x_A, y_A) - \overline{U}_A]$$

$$-\delta_1(\overline{x}_A + \overline{x}_B - \overline{x}) - \delta_2(\overline{y}_A + \overline{y}_B - \overline{y})$$

The problem for individual A is now solved by deriving with respect to each goods.

$$\frac{\partial L_A}{\partial x_A} = \frac{\partial U_A(x_A, y_A)}{\partial x_A} - \mu_1 = 0$$

$$\frac{\partial L_A}{\partial y_A} = \frac{\partial U_A(x_A, y_A)}{\partial y_A} - \mu_2 = 0$$

$$\frac{\partial L_A}{\partial x_B} = -\lambda \frac{\partial U_B(x_B, y_B)}{\partial x_B} - \mu_1 = 0$$

$$\frac{\partial L_A}{\partial y_B} = -\lambda \frac{\partial U_B(x_B, y_B)}{\partial y_B} - \mu_2 = 0$$

From the above first-order conditions we obtain that:

$$\frac{\partial U_A(x_A,y_A)}{\partial x_A} = MU_{x_A} \; ; \; \frac{\partial U_A(x_A,y_A)}{\partial y_A} = MU_{y_A}$$

and we also know that

$$\frac{\partial U_B(x_B,y_B)}{\partial x_B} = MU_{x_B} \; ; \; \frac{\partial U_B(x_B,y_B)}{\partial y_B} = MU_{y_B}$$

Moreover, by dividing in the first-order conditions the first equation by the second, we have that:

$$\frac{MU_{x_A}}{MU_{y_A}} = \frac{\mu_1}{\mu_2}$$

and dividing in the first-order conditions the third equation by the fourth one, we obtain that:

$$\frac{MU_{x_B}}{MU_{y_B}} = \frac{\mu_1}{\mu_2}$$

This means that:

$$\frac{MU_{x_A}}{MU_{y_A}} = \frac{MU_{x_B}}{MU_{y_B}} = \frac{\mu_1}{\mu_2} = MRS_A = MRS_B$$

If we solve the problem of individual B we obtain the following first-order conditions:

$$\frac{\partial L_B}{\partial x_B} = \frac{\partial U_B(x_B,y_B)}{\partial x_B} - \delta_1 = 0$$

$$\frac{\partial L_B}{\partial y_B} = \frac{\partial U_B(x_B,y_B)}{\partial y_B} - \delta_2 = 0$$

$$\frac{\partial L_B}{\partial x_A} = -\gamma \frac{\partial U_A(x_A,y_A)}{\partial x_A} - \delta_1 = 0$$

$$\frac{\partial L_B}{\partial y_A} = -\gamma \frac{\partial U_A(x_A, y_A)}{\partial y_A} - \delta_2 = 0$$

from which we have:

$$\frac{MU_{x_B}}{MU_{y_B}} = \frac{\delta_1}{\delta_2}; \frac{MU_{x_A}}{MU_{x_B}} = \frac{\delta_1}{\delta_2}$$

All this means that:

$$\frac{MU_{x_B}}{MU_{y_B}} = \frac{MU_{x_A}}{MU_{x_B}} = \frac{\delta_1}{\delta_2} = MRS_A = MRS_B$$

1.1.2 GE Model with Production: 2 Consumers and 2 Producers

1.1.2.1 Approach from the Agents as Producers

Assume a very simple economy in which there are two individuals A and B who produce and consume two goods (x, y). In contrast with the pure exchange model, here, each individual will have to produce amounts of goods behaving as producer.

$$\Pi_A = x_A P_x + y_A P_y - w L_A - r k_A$$

s. to $0 = \phi(x_A, y_A)$

$$0 = \phi(x_A, y_A, L_A, k_A)$$

and the auxiliary Lagrange function will be:

$$L(x_A, y_A, \lambda) = x_A P_x + y_A P_y - w L_A - r k_A - \lambda[-\phi(x_A, y_A)]$$

$$\frac{\partial L}{\partial x_A} = P_x + \lambda \frac{\partial \phi(x_A, y_A)}{\partial x_A} = 0$$

$$\frac{\partial L}{\partial y_A} = P_y + \lambda \frac{\partial \phi(x_A, y_A)}{\partial y_A} = 0$$

$$\frac{\partial L}{\partial \lambda} = \phi(x_A, y_A) = 0$$

$$\frac{\partial L}{\partial L_A} = -w + \lambda \frac{\partial \phi(x_A, y_A)}{\partial L_A} = 0$$

$$\frac{\partial L}{\partial k_A} = -r + \lambda \frac{\partial \phi(x_A, y_A)}{\partial k_A} = 0$$

The above first-order conditions may give rise to the following statements. From the first two equations we obtain that:

$$\frac{\partial \phi(x_A, y_A)/\partial x_A}{\partial \phi(x_A, y_A)/\partial y_A} = \frac{P_x}{P_y} = (MRT_x^y)_A = \frac{MU_x}{MU_y}$$

output-output marginal rate of transformation.

The quotient of the prices of outputs (P_x, P_y) is equal to the Marginal Rate of Transformation between products (x, y), in short, a product of the tangency between a curve of product transformation and an income or budget restriction.

From the last two equations we have that:

$$\frac{\partial \phi(x_A, y_A)/\partial L_A}{\partial \phi(x_A, y_A)/\partial k_A} = \frac{w}{r} = (MRTS_L^k) = \left(\frac{MP_L}{MP_k}\right)_A$$

a marginal rate of technical substitution whose immediate interpretation is the weighed marginal productivity law. In other words, the quotient of marginal products of inputs is equal to the quotient of the input prices. In short, a tangency point between isocost and an isoquant restriction.

From the first and fourth equations we have that:

$$\frac{\partial \phi(x_A, y_A)/\partial x_A}{\partial \phi(x_A, y_A)/\partial L_A} = \frac{-P_x}{w} = (IORS_x^L)_A$$

an input-output rates of substitution and at the same time a rate of substitution between second and fifth equations:

$$\frac{\partial \phi(x_A, y_A)/\partial y_A}{\partial \phi(x_A, y_A)/\partial k_A} = \frac{-P_y}{r} = (IORS_y^k)_A$$

The two rates above require equality of equilibrium between the input-output rates of substitution for consumer A between output x with input L and output y with input k.

Following the same process for individual B as for individual A, we obtain the results below:

$$\frac{\partial\phi(x_B,y_B)/\partial x_B}{\partial\phi(x_B,y_B)/\partial y_B} = \frac{P_x}{P_y} = (MRT_x^y)_B$$

$$\frac{\partial\phi(x_B,y_B)/\partial L_B}{\partial\phi(x_B,y_B)/\partial k_B} = \frac{w}{r} = (MRTS_L^k)_B$$

$$\frac{\partial\phi(x_B,y_B)/\partial x_B}{\partial\phi(x_B,y_B)/\partial L_B} = \frac{-P_x}{w} = (IORS_x^L)_B$$

$$\frac{\partial\phi(x_B,y_B)/\partial y_B}{\partial\phi(x_B,y_B)/\partial k_B} = \frac{-P_y}{r} = (IORS_y^k)_B$$

In the Theory of Equilibrium, profit is maximized while cost is minimized for a technology and the output is maximized for certain costs. The last problem is similar to the problem of utility maximization for a given income and therefore, the maximization of amounts x and y for a given cost can be represented. This means that:

$$(MRT_x^y)_A = \frac{P_x}{P_y} = \left(\frac{MU_x}{MU_y}\right)_A = MRS_A$$

in addition:

$$(MRT_x^y)_B = \frac{P_x}{P_y} = \left(\frac{MU_x}{MU_y}\right)_B = MRS_B$$

and therefore, in equilibrium for both:

$$MRT_A = MRT_B = MRS_A = MRS_B$$

Moreover, in equilibrium it will be verified that:

$$MRTS_A = MRTS_B = w/r$$

and that:

$$(IORS_x^L)_A = (IORS_x^L)_B = -\frac{P_x}{w}$$

$$(IORS_y^k)_A = (IORS_y^k)_B = -\frac{P_y}{r}$$

In general equilibrium, for the case of two consumers-producers (A, B) and two goods (x, y), there will be equilibrium when the global equilibrium condition is verified:

$$(MRT_x^y)_A = (MRT_x^y)_B = MRS_A = MRS_B = \frac{P_x}{P_y}$$

Moreover, as:

$$\frac{(IORS_x^L)_A}{(IORS_y^k)_A} = \frac{P_x}{P_y}\frac{r}{w} = \frac{(IORS_x^L)_B}{(IORS_y^k)_B} = \frac{P_x}{P_y}\frac{r}{w}$$

$$\frac{P_x(IORS_y^k)_A}{P_y(IORS_x^L)_A} = \frac{w}{r} = MRTS_A = MRTS_B$$

the following is satisfied:

$$MRTS_A = MRTS_B = \frac{w}{r}$$

equilibrium condition in the output.
   Besides:

$$MRS_A = MRS_B = \frac{P_x}{P_y}$$

equilibrium condition in consumption.
   This model enables us to determine the equilibrium prices (P_x, P_y, w, r), in other words, the price vector which guarantees that the demand surpluses for the goods x, y equal zero.

1.1.2.2 Approach from the Agents as Consumers

Assuming an economy with two individuals A and B who produce and consume two goods (x, y), these individuals produce these goods from a multiproduct technology ψ (x,y) = 0 with the aim of maximizing their utility:

   U_i (x_i, y_i); with i = A, B

The following problem can be exposed for individual A:

   max U_A (x_A, y_A)

s. to $U_B(x_B, y_B) = \overline{U}$

$0 = \psi(x, y)$

The Lagrangian of this problem can be written as:

$$L_A = U_A(x_A, y_A) - \lambda[U_B(x_B, y_B) - \overline{U}] - \mu[-\psi(x, y)]$$

The first-order conditions of this auxiliary Lagrange function are:

$$\frac{\partial L_A}{\partial x_A} = \frac{\partial U_A(x_A, y_A)}{\partial x_A} - \mu \frac{\partial \psi(x, y)}{\partial x_A} = 0$$

$$\frac{\partial L_A}{\partial y_A} = \frac{\partial U_A(x_A, y_A)}{\partial y_A} - \mu \frac{\partial \psi(x, y)}{\partial y_A} = 0$$

$$\frac{\partial L_A}{\partial x_B} = -\lambda \frac{\partial U_B(x_B, y_B)}{\partial x_B} + \mu \frac{\partial \psi(x, y)}{\partial x_B} = 0$$

$$\frac{\partial L_A}{\partial y_B} = -\lambda \frac{\partial U_B(x_B, y_B)}{\partial y_B} + \mu \frac{\partial \psi(x, y)}{\partial y_B} = 0$$

where $x = x_A + x_B$ and

$$\mu \frac{\partial \psi(x, y)}{\partial x_A} = \frac{\partial \psi(x_A + x_B, y)}{\partial x_A} = \frac{\partial U_A(x_A, y_A)}{\partial x_A}$$

and where $y = y_A + y_B$;

$$\frac{\partial \psi(x, y_A + y_B)}{\partial y_A} = \frac{\partial U_A(x_A, y_A)}{\partial y_A}$$

Therefore, we can split the statements above into:

$$(MRT_x^y)_A = \left(\frac{MU_x}{MU_y}\right)_A = MRS_A$$

From the remaining first-order equations, it is possible to write:

$$(MRT_x^y)_B = \left(\frac{MU_x}{MU_y}\right)_B = MRS_B$$

The marginal rate of substitution for individuals A and B must be equal to the marginal rate of transformation between products. This means that the rate at which each individual is willing to replace good x with good y must be equal to the rate at which it is technologically feasible to transform a good x into a good y. However, this must not be understood as a transformation of x into y (of wheat into guns, for example), but that the resources used to produce are employed in the production of x until the marginal rates of substitution of both goods are equal for each individual. This means that there will not be any possibility to increase this individual's utility without affecting the other individual's utility.

1.2
First Stage of GE: From the Invisible Hand to the Walrasian Notion

In 1776, Adam Smith, a Scottish professor of Moral Philosophy, published "An Inquiry into the Nature and Causes of the Wealth of Nations". This work is based on the idea of a system of allocation which generates an equilibrium with desired properties where consumers and producers take their economic decisions separately seeking the maximization of their individual welfare, and where all the relevant economic information is transmitted only by the prices of the goods and services exchanged. We will understand the equilibrium as a state in which agents lack the incentives to behave in a different way, in other words, a state which tends to perpetuate unless some basic parameters of the model change: the individuals' preferences, the assignment of resources and the technology.

To this point, we have shown very simplified versions of GE of the type 2 consumers and 2 producers. With a higher number of consumers and producers, this model will be extended to more economies with few restrictions by introducing *numerarie* and fiduciary money. These findings are apparent at the first stage of GE, a stage at which the problem of the existence of GE is presented but is not solved.

1.2.1 The Walrasian GE Model with Production

In 1874, León Walras, a French maths professor published "Eléments d'Economie Politique Pure oú Théorie de la Richesse Sociale". In his work, he presented the behavior of individual agents as maximizers of the target function (welfare and profit function) subjected to some restrictions (institutional and technical restrictions as well as assignment of resources restrictions), which enabled him to obtain demand and supply functions for all the goods and services which only depend on the price vector of the economy.

Consider an economy with L consumers, each of whom has a utility function of the type U (x,y) since there are only two goods in the economy. Each subject behaves now as a maximizer:

max U (x, y)

s. to $x\,P_x + y\,P_y = R$

where $R = w + k\,r + A$

Being:

w = wage (each individual sells a labor unit);

k = machinery owned by the individual;

r = price of machinery service;

A = subject's share in the profits of the various businesses.

In competitive equilibrium, the profits are zero. Therefore, A=0.

Taking this into account, the individual demand functions can be expressed as follows:

$x^d = d_x\,(P_x, P_y, w, r)$

$y^d = d_y\,(P_x, P_y, w, r)$

(k is not explicit for being a parameter).
    Aggregating for L individuals we obtain the following functions:

$X^d = D_x\,(P_x, P_y, w, r)$

$Y^d = D_y\,(P_x, P_y, w, r)$

As far as the firms are concerned, each one maximizes its profit.
    In sector x:

max $\pi_x = f\,(l_x, k_x)\,P_x - (x\,l_x + r\,k_x)$

From here we obtain input demand and output supply functions x:

$l_x^{\,d} = l_x\,(w, r, P_x)$

$k_x^{\,d} = k_x\,(w, r, P_x)$

$x^S = S_x\,(w, r, P_x)$

Similarly, in sector y we obtain the individual input demand function and supply function of output y:

$$l_y^d = l_y (w, r, P_y)$$

$$k_y^d = k_y (w, r, P_y)$$

$$y^S = S_y (w, r, P_y)$$

By aggregating, we obtain:

$$L^d = \Sigma_x l_x^d + \Sigma_y l_y^d = D_L (P_x, P_y, w, r, N_x, N_y)$$

$$K^d = \Sigma_x k_x^d + \Sigma_y k_y^d = D_L (P_x, P_y, w, r, N_x, N_y)$$

To express the input demands in this way, we assume that all the firms of each sector are equal: there are N_x firms in sector x and N_y firms in sector y.

It is also possible to obtain by aggregation the following supply functions:

$$X^S = \Sigma_x S_x = S_x (P_x, w, r, N_x)$$

$$Y^S = \Sigma_Y S_Y = S_Y (P_Y, w, r, N_Y)$$

N_x and N_y appear because all the firms are equal in equilibrium for each sector.

The GE situation can now be described by a system of six equations and six unknown quantities:

$$D_x = S_x$$

$$D_y = S_y$$

$$D_L = \overline{L} \ (\overline{L} \ \text{fixed})$$

$$D_k = \overline{K} \ (\overline{K} \ \text{fixed})$$

$$\pi_x = (P_x, w, r) = 0$$

$$\pi_y = (P_Y, w, r) = 0 \tag{1.1}$$

There are six equations and six unknown quantities: $(P_x, P_y, w, r, N_x, N_y)$. Nevertheless, one equation is a linear combination of the others.

1.2.1.1 Walras' Law

We know that for each consumer $\Sigma d \equiv \Sigma$ fact.sup.; by aggregating for all consumers we have that:

$$D_x P_x + D_y P_y \equiv \overline{L} w + \overline{K} r$$

Predicted purchases $\equiv$ consumers' total income

In other words, profits become null.

For the firms the following is satisfied:

$$S_x\, P_x + S_y\, P_y \equiv D_L\, w + D_k\, r$$

Predicted output sales $\equiv$ Predicted input purchases

Where the profits become null.

The above statements can be rewritten as follows:

$$D_x\, P_x + D_y\, P_y - \overline{L}w - \overline{K}r = 0$$

$$S_x\, P_x + S_y\, P_y - D_L\, w - D_k\, r = 0$$

By subtracting these two statements, we obtain:

$$(D_x - S_x)\, P_x + (D_y - S_y)\, P_y + (D_L - \overline{L})\, w + (D_k - \overline{K})\, r = 0$$

from which we have that in system (1.1) the first four equations are interrelated if three markets are in equilibrium, the fourth is also:

If all the demand and supply functions are degree-zero homogeneous (from here onwards D0H) in (p^*, w, r) and given that the profit functions are also D0H provided that $\pi = 0$ in (p^*, w, r), we can eliminate an unknown quantity if we multiply all the prices by $1/P_x$, so the system would result into:

$$D_x\left(1, \frac{P_y}{P_x}, \frac{w}{P_x}, \frac{r}{P_x}\right) = S_x\left(1, \frac{w}{P_x}, \frac{r}{P_x}, N_x\right)$$

$$D_y\left(1, \frac{P_y}{P_x}, \frac{w}{P_x}, \frac{r}{P_x}\right) = S_y\left(\frac{P_y}{P_x}, \frac{w}{P_x}, \frac{r}{P_x}, N_y\right)$$

$$D_L\left(1, \frac{P_y}{P_x}, \frac{w}{P_x}, \frac{r}{P_x}, N_x, N_y\right) = \overline{L}$$

$$D_k\left(1, \frac{P_y}{P_x}, \frac{w}{P_x}, \frac{r}{P_x}, N_x, N_y\right) = \overline{K}$$

$$\pi_x\left(1, \frac{w}{P_x}, \frac{r}{P_x}\right) = 0$$

$$\pi_x\left(\frac{P_y}{P_x}, \frac{w}{P_x}, \frac{r}{P_x}\right) = 0$$

which allows us to obtain –assuming that there is a solution- the following equilibrium values:

$$\left(\frac{P_y}{P_x}\right)^*, \left(\frac{w}{P_x}\right)^*, \left(\frac{r}{P_x}\right)^*, N_x^*, N_y^*$$

from which the values x^*, y^*, L_x^*, L_y^*, ..., etc. can be inferred.

1.2.2 Walrasian GE Model with Production and *Numerarie* Money

How does money affect the nature of competitive equilibrium?
Individuals' money, which will be expressed as m, can be considered as one more good, therefore:

$$U = U(\vec{x}, m)$$

where $\vec{x}$ is the vector of consumed goods and m is the monetary wages.

$$\max U(\vec{x}, m)$$

s. to $\vec{P} \cdot \vec{x} + m = R$

From here, we can obtain the following demand functions:

$$x = d_x(\vec{P}, R)$$

$$m = d_m(\vec{P}, R)$$

where all the prices of goods are measured in money ($P_m = 1$).
    On the whole, these functions are not D0H in $\vec{P}$ and R, and neither is $d_m(\vec{P}, R)$ D1H (degree-one homogeneous) in $\vec{P}$ and R. However, they should satisfy these properties. How would we get this?
    Assuming utility functions of the type:

$$U(\vec{x}, m) = [\phi(\vec{x})]^\alpha m^\beta$$

$$U_{\vec{x}} / U_m = P/1$$

$$U_{\vec{x}} = \alpha \phi(\vec{x})^{\alpha-1} \phi'(\vec{x}) m^\beta$$

$$U_m = \beta \phi(\vec{x})^\alpha m^{\beta-1}$$

$$U_{\vec{x}} / U_m = [\alpha \phi'(\vec{x}) m] / [\beta \phi(\vec{x})] = P$$

$$\left.\begin{array}{l} \dfrac{\alpha}{\beta} \dfrac{\phi'(\vec{x})}{\phi(\vec{x})} m = P \\[2em] \vec{P} \cdot \vec{x} + m = R \end{array}\right\} \tag{1.2}$$

assume that $\vec{P}$ and R are multiplied by λ, then we will have the following system:

$$\left. \begin{array}{l} \dfrac{\alpha}{\beta}\,\dfrac{\phi'(\vec{x})}{\phi(\vec{x})}\,m = \lambda P \\[3mm] \lambda\vec{P}\cdot\vec{x} + m = \lambda R \end{array} \right\} \tag{1.3}$$

Let's define now the variable $v = m/\lambda$, in this case it is possible to write:

$$\left. \begin{array}{l} \dfrac{\alpha}{\beta}\,\dfrac{\phi'(\vec{x})}{\phi(\vec{x})}\,\lambda v = \lambda P \\[3mm] \lambda\vec{P}\cdot\vec{x} + \lambda v = \lambda R \end{array} \right\} \tag{1.4}$$

System (1.4) is equal to (1.2) at all, except for the fact that m in (1.2) is replaced with v in (1.4). Therefore, the solutions of both systems are numerically identical. If (x^*, m^*) is the solution for system (1.2), the solution for system (1.4) will be (x^*, v^*) where $m^* = v^*$.

Which one is the solution which corresponds to (1.3)?. System (1.3) is completely equal to (1.4), except for the fact that while m is written in (1.3), λv ($m = \lambda v$) is written in (1.4).

If $v = v^*$, $m = \lambda v^*$,

and as $m^* = v^*$, it follows that $m = \lambda m^*$.

Therefore, the solution for (1.3) is $(x^*, \lambda m^*)$. In other words, if $\vec{P}$ and R are multiplied by λ, the volume of demanded wages is multiplied by λ and the demands for goods are not altered.

Therefore, $d_x(\vec{P}, R)$ is D0H in $\vec{P}$ and R and $d_m(\vec{P}, R)$ is D1H in $\vec{P}$ and R.

The Walrasian system results as follows:

$$D_{x_1}\left(P_1,...,P_n, w, r, M_1,..., M_{\overline{L}}\right) = S_{x_1}\left(P_1, w, r, N_1\right)$$

$$\dotfill$$

$$D_{x_n}\left(P_1,...,P_n, w, r, M_1,..., M_{\overline{L}}\right) = S_{x_n}\left(P_n, w, r, N_n\right)$$

$$D_L\left(P_1,...,P_n, w, r, N_1,..., N_n\right) = \overline{L}$$

$$D_k\left(P_1,...,P_n, w, r, N_1,..., N_n\right) = \overline{k}$$

$$\pi_{x_1}\left(P_1, w, r\right) = 0$$

$$\dotfill$$

$$\pi_{x_n}\left(P_n, w, r\right) = 0$$

$$D_M\left(P_1,...,P_n, w, r, M_1,..., M_{\overline{L}}\right) = M$$

where M_1, ..., $M_{\overline{L}}$ show the initial money assignments for each subject.

Each subject's income is $R = lw + kr + M_{-1} + A$, where A is the share in business profits. In equilibrium $A = 0$, R is D1H in w, r and M_{-1}, from which follows that the demand functions are D0H in $(\vec{P}, w, r, \overline{M})$.

Supply functions are D0H in ($\vec{P}$, w, r). We also assume that the companies do not make profits. Walras' Law is satisfied since:

$$P\ D_x + D_M \equiv (\overline{L}w + \overline{k}r) + M + \pi \qquad (1.5)$$

Planned expenses	+	Retained Payment	$\equiv$	Income (planned) from production inputs	+	Inherited Monetary payment	+	Income from profit shares

$$P\ S_x \equiv (D_L w + D_k r) + \pi \qquad (1.6)$$

Planned sales	$\equiv$	Planned purchases	+	Remnant

Rewriting (1.5) and (1.6) we have that:

$$P \cdot\ D_x + D_M - \overline{L}w\ +\ \overline{k}r\ - M \equiv \pi$$

$$P \cdot\ S_x + D_L w - D_k r \equiv \pi$$

From which follows that:

$$P\ (D_x - S_x) + (D_L - \overline{L}) + r\ (D_k - \overline{k}) + (D_M - M) = 0$$

which again implies that Walras' Law is satisfied.

If goods, labor and capital markets are in equilibrium, the money market will be too.

A surplus in the demand for goods (with markets of inputs in equilibrium) implies a surplus in money supply (people want to replace money with goods: the holding of cash (predicted) is reduced and it is used to buy goods. However, a surplus in goods supply may be associated with a surplus in the demand for money: people try to accumulate money by not buying goods.

Therefore, the system has a redundant equation. There are $2n + 3$ independent equations and $2n + 2$ unknown quantities ($P_1,\dots P_n$, N_1, N_2, ..., N_n, w, r) which can be obtained. Thus, in this system we obtain the number of companies of each sector and the monetary prices (i.e., absolute prices).

Note that, as we have here defined, the monetary equilibrium $D_M = M$ does not imply that the monetary quantity of wages demanded by each subject remains invariable throughout time. On the whole we have that $d_m \neq M_{-1}$ for the different subjects. We have just characterized a situation of temporary (or transitory) equilibrium. If it happens that $d_m = M_{-1}$, we will have the "permanent" or stationary equilibrium solution for every subject.

1.2.3 Walrasian GE Model with Production and Circulating and Fiduciary Money

Each subject maximizes his utility $U(x_1, \dots x_n)$ under a budget restriction of the type:

$$\sum_{i=1}^{n} P_i x_i + m = R + m_0$$

where m accounts for the monetary wages necessary to finance the transactions of the period and m_0 is the initial holding of money. We also assume that:

$$m = \alpha \sum_{i=1}^{M} P_i x_i$$

which means that the amount of money demanded is strictly proportional to the transaction values. It is assumed that α is an institutional parameter.

The budget restriction can be expressed as:

$$(1+\alpha) \, \Sigma_i \, P_i x_i = R + m_0$$

or:

$$\Sigma_i \, P_i x_i = (R + m_0) \, / \, (1+\alpha)$$

Maximizing utility regularly, we obtain the demand functions:

$$d_i \, [P_1, \, ..., \, P_n, \, (R + m_0) \, / \, (1+\alpha)]; \, i = 1, \, ..., \, n$$

which are D0H in $(P_1, \, ..., \, P_n; \, (R + m_0) \, / \, (1+\alpha))$.

We make $R = w + kr + A$, where k is the subject's assignment of money (assumed as fixed) and A is the addition of his shares in the profits of the existing companies.

Statement A is a D1H function in $P_1, ... \, P_n$, w, r and m_0. We can say that d_i is D0H in the same variables. The aggregate demands will be:

$$D_i \, (P_1, \, ..., \, P_n, \, w, \, r, \, \vec{m}_0 \,)$$

Also individual money demand functions:

$$d_m \, (P_1, \, ..., \, P_n, \, w, \, r, \, m_0) \equiv \alpha \, \Sigma_i \, P_i d_i \, (P_1, \, ..., \, P_n, \, w, \, r, \, m_0)$$

which are, obviously, D1H in $(P_1, \, ..., \, P_n; w, \, r \, y \, m_0)$.

The aggregate money demand function is:

$$D_M \, (P_1, ... \, P_n, \, w, \, r, \, m_0^1, ..., m_0^{L^s} \,)$$

which is D1H in $(\vec{P}, \, w, \, r, \, \vec{m}_0 \,)$.

The general equilibrium system can be exposed as follows:

$$D_i \, (\vec{P}, \, w, \, r, \, \vec{m}_0 \,) = S_i \, (P_i, \, w, \, r, \, N_i); \, i = 1, \, ..., \, n$$

$$D_L \, (\vec{P}, \, w, \, r, \, \vec{N} \,) = L^s$$

$$D_k \, (\vec{P}, \, w, \, r, \, \vec{N} \,) = k^s$$

$$\pi_i \, (P_i, \, w, \, r) = 0$$

$$D_M (\vec{P}, w, r, \vec{m}_0) = M^s$$

This system satisfies Walras' Law since, by aggregating the world budget restrictions we have that:

$$\Sigma_i P_i D_i + D_M \equiv (L^s w + k^s r) + M^s + \pi \tag{1.7}$$

Planned expenses		Retained payment		Income from the production inputs		Inherited Monetary payment = money supply		Income derived from profit shares
	+		$\equiv$		+		+	

In addition, by aggregating the balances of all the companies, we have that:

$$\Sigma_i P_i S_i \equiv (D_L w + D_k r) + \pi \tag{1.8}$$

Planned income		Planned purchases		Remnant
	$\equiv$		+	

Rewriting (1.7) and (1.8) we have that:

$$\Sigma_i P_i D_i + D_M - L^s w - k^s r - M^s \equiv \pi$$

$$\Sigma_i P_i S_i - D_L w - D_k r \equiv \pi$$

from which it follows that:

$$\Sigma_i P_i (D_i - S_i) + w (D_L - L^s) + r (D_k - k^s) + (D_M - M^s) \equiv 0$$

which implies that the Walras Rule is satisfied:

There are $2n+3$ equations of which $2n+2$ are independent. The unknown quantities are $2n+2$:

$$(P_1, ..., P_n, w, r, N_1, ...,N_n)$$

money prices   number of
=   companies
"absolute"
prices

"Initially" it is possible to solve the system.

What happens if money supply duplicates? That is to say M^s, $m_0^1,..., m_0^{\bar{L}}$ are multiplied by two and then we have the following system:

$$D_i (\vec{P}, w, r, 2\vec{m}_0) = S_i (P_i, w, r, N_i); \ i = 1, ..., n$$

$$D_L (\vec{P}, w, r, \vec{N}) = L^s$$

$$D_k (\vec{P}, w, r, \vec{N}) = k^s$$

$$\pi_i (P_i, w, r) = 0$$

$$D_M(\vec{P}, w, r, 2\vec{m}_0) = 2\,M^s$$

This system differs from the one above only in the fact that where M^S appeared in the former, in the new system $2M^S$ appears. Moreover, where we expressed $\vec{m}_0$ in the previous system, in the new system we have $2\vec{m}_0$. Assuming that $(\vec{P}^*, w^*, r^*, \vec{N}^*)$ is the solution of the initial system, now we will prove that $(2\vec{P}^*, 2w^*, 2r^*, \vec{N}^*)$ is the solution to this system in which we have duplicated money supply. In order to prove this we define:

$$q_i = P_i/2;\ \varpi = w/2;\ \rho = r/2;$$

from which it follows that:

$$P_i = 2q_i\ ;\ w = 2\varpi\ ;\ r = 2\rho;$$

Substituting these values in the system with duplicated money supply, we can write:

$$D_i(2\vec{q}, 2\varpi, 2\rho, 2\vec{m}_0) = S_i(2q_i, 2\varpi, 2\rho, N_i);\ i = 1, ..., n$$

$$D_L(2\vec{q}, 2\varpi, 2\rho, \vec{N}) = L^s$$

$$D_k(2\vec{q}, 2\varpi, 2\rho, \vec{N}) = k^s$$

$$\pi_i(2q_i, 2\varpi, 2\rho) = 0$$

$$D_M(2\vec{q}, 2\varpi, 2\rho, 2\vec{m}_0) = 2\,M^s$$

We know that $D_i(\cdot)$ is D0H in the initial prices and assignments of money; $S_i(\cdot)$ is D0H in prices; $D_L(\cdot)$ and $D_k(\cdot)$ are D0H in prices and $\pi_i(\cdot)$ is D1H in prices; $D_M(\cdot)$ is D1H in initial prices and money assignments.

Therefore, the system with duplicated money supply can be reduced to another one which is identical to the non-duplicated money supply system, with the only particularity that, where P_i, w, r appeared, now we write q_i, ϖ, ρ. For this reason, the solutions are identical. In other words:

$$P_i^* = q_i^*, i = 1, ..., n$$

$$w^* = \varpi^*$$

$$r^* = \rho^*$$

N^* common for both.

Given that $q_i = P_i/2$; if we make $q_i = P_i^*$, it follows that $P_i = 2\,P_i^*$
    Given that $\varpi = w/2$; if we make $\varpi = w^*$, it follows that $w = 2w^*$
    Given that $\rho = r/2$; if we make $\rho = r^*$, it follows that $r = 2r^*$.
Therefore, the solution of the Walrasian system with duplicated money supply is:

$$P_i = 2P_i^*;\ i = 1, ..., n$$

$$w = 2w^*$$

$r = 2r^*$

$N = N^*$

All prices are multiplied by two and the "real" variables do not change. In short, we have proved that money is neutral in the GE Model.

1.3
Second Stage of GE: From the Walrasian Notion to the Existence Demonstration

This stage tries to answer the indicated weakness: the equality between the number of linearly independent equations and the number of unknown quantities does not guarantee either the existence of a solution or, even less, that the solution implies non negative prices. With this purpose, the use of the convexity concept and topology (the Brouwer and Kakutani fixed point theories) is required, and this constitutes an essential contribution of the leading works by Debreu (1951), Arrow (1951) and Arrow-Debreu (1954), which culminate with Debreu (1959). Which results are obtained from this second stage?

A set of sufficient conditions which guarantee the existence of GE and which, as regards the essential points, are concerned with the continuity and homogeneity of the surplus demand functions as well as with satisfying the so-called Walras' Law.

1.3.1 The GE Model Extended by Arrow-Debreu

As the Walras Model corresponds to the first stage, the Arrow-Debreu Model corresponds to the second stage. This model has the very desired property of guaranteeing the existence of general competitive equilibrium on the basis of very few fundamental assumptions. These assumptions are the following:

i) Each consumer has an initial assignment of goods $x_i \subset \mathbb{R}^n_+$, formed by a compact and convex set of goods, and a final assignment of goods – after exchanging – or demand which we will denominate x_i^d, in other words:

$x_i^d = Z_i + x_i$

where $Z_i = x_i^d - x_i$ is the surplus of net demand.

ii) Each consumer has a set of preferences which guarantees the existence of a utility function defined for surpluses of net demand such as:

$U_i = U_i (Z_i)$

and such that $x_i^d + x_i \geq 0$, in other words the Z_i are limited at the bottom by x_i.

iii) Each utility function U_i is continuous in Z_i

iv) Non-local saturation, that is to say, given Z_i and $\varepsilon > 0$, there is a $\overline{Z}_i$ such that:

$0 < |\overline{Z}_i - Z_i| < \varepsilon; U (\overline{Z}_i) < U (Z_i)$

v) Each utility function U_i is quasi-concave, in other words: for $\overline{Z}_i \neq Z_i$ y $U(Z_i) \geq U(\overline{Z}_i)$, then, it must be verified that:

$U(t\, Z_i + (1 - t)\, \overline{Z}_i) \geq U(\overline{Z}_i); \forall t \in (0.1)$.

That is to say, sets $\{Z_i \in \mathbb{R}^n_+ / U_i(Z_i) \geq a\}$ are strictly convex in a and the indifference curves do not have flat sides.

vi) The consumer is rational, in other words:

max $U_i(Z_i)$

s.to $p\, x_i^d - p\, x_i \leq \Sigma_k A_k + w + k\, r$

where p accounts for the price vector of the goods; A_k is the profit share i-th of the consumer in the i-th company and no dividends are retained by the companies; w is each consumer's wage; k accounts for the machinery owned by each individual and r is the price of the machinery services.

vii) Each company operates within its set of technical production possibilities $x_k \in X_k$, where each item x_k accounts for the feasible net production.

viii) Set x_k is compact, in other words, x_k is closed and bounded for all $\alpha > 0$ and $\alpha x_k \in X_k$.

ix) Set X_k is strictly convex.

x) Null production is possible. In other words: $0 \in X_k$.

xi) Production is not free; every activity requires inputs:

$X_k \cap \mathbb{R}^n_+ = \{0\}$

xii) Production is irreversible since we cannot obtain inputs from outputs:

$X_k \cap (-X_k) = \{0\}$

With the previous assumptions, it is possible to write:

$\vec{X} = \Sigma_k\, x_k$

as a representation of the vector which indicates the feasible net production:

$\vec{Z} = \Sigma_i\, Z_i$

as a representation of the vector which indicates the surplus of net demand.
The equilibrium is defined as:

$\vec{X} = \vec{Z}$

and the demand surplus function $E(\vec{P})$

$E(\vec{P}) = \Sigma_i\, Z_i(\vec{P}, R_i) - \Sigma_k\, x_k(\vec{P})$

or

$E(\vec{P}) = \Sigma_i\, x_i^d(\vec{P}, R_i) - \Sigma_i\, x_i - \Sigma_k\, x_k(\vec{P})$

Under the previous assumptions, from the Arrow-Debreu model the following properties of the demand functions can be guaranteed:

i) Demand functions $x^d_i(\vec{P}, R_i)$ are continuous in the prices and for each price vector $\vec{P}$, the consumer has only one demand response.

ii) Demand functions $x^d_i(\vec{P}, R_i)$ are degree-zero homogeneous, in other words, there is not monetary illusion.

iii) Walras's Law is verified for each price vector $\vec{P}$ since the maximum to be chosen is above budget line $\vec{P} x^d = R$.

Similarly, the following properties of the production sets can be guaranteed:

i) In the problem:

$$\max \vec{P} x_k$$

s. to $x_k \in X_k$

$x_k \in X_k$ is the only solution to the maximization problem of the firm.

ii) X_k is compact (in other words, closed and bounded). The production function with efficient technique exists and is unique.

iii) $X_k(\vec{P})$ is continuos with respect to price vector $\vec{P}$ given the previous axioms and properties for consumers and products.

Demand surplus function $E(\vec{P})$ has the following properties:

i) For each price vector $\vec{P}$ there is a unique level of $E(\vec{P})$ since the response of the optimization process from consumers and producers is only one and well defined.

ii) Function $E(\vec{P})$ is degree-zero homogeneous since both the consumer's demand and the producer's supply is degree-zero homogeneous. In other words, there is not monetary illusion.

iii) For all level of prices $\vec{P}$ Walras' Law is verified and therefore:

$$\vec{P} \cdot E(\vec{P}) = 0$$

iv) Demand surplus function $E(\vec{P})$ is continuous in price vector $\vec{P}$.

In order to prove the existence of GE in the model Arrow-Debreu provides de following theorem.

1.3.1.1 Existence Theorem (Canonic Approach)

If $E(\vec{P})$ is a continuous degree-zero homogeneous function and satisfies Walras's Law, then there is at least one equilibrium price vector.

1.3.1.2 Demonstration (Canonic Approach: Arrow-Debreu)

This is guaranteed under the properties of the demand functions and of the production sets which aggregate the properties of demand surplus function $E(\vec{P})$.

1.3.1.3 Existence Theorem (Game Theory Approach)

A game of complete information whose space of game strategies S_i is complete and convex for each player $i \in N$, whose payment function $P_i(s) \in R$ is defined, continuous and limited for all $s \in S$ y $\forall i \in N$ and such that:

$P_i(S_1, S_{i-1}, t_i, S_{i+1}, ..., S_n)$ is concave with respect to $t_i \in S_i$, $\forall i \in N$

and which satisfies the following game rules:

R1 Players are not able to enter into binding agreements.

R2 Each player's strategic choice is made prior to the game agreement and the strategic choices made by the rest of the players are unknown. This choice has at least one equilibrium point.

About this theorem, see Friedman's demonstration (1986).

1.3.1.4 Existence Theorems (Topological Approach: Brower and Kakutani)

If $E(\vec{P})$ is a continuous degree-zero homogeneity function and it satisfies Walras' Law, then there is at least one equilibrium price vector.

1.3.1.5 Existence Demonstration

If $E(\vec{P})$ is degree-zero homogeneous, there is not generality loss if we standardize prices, in other words, if we have now a set S:

$$S = \{\vec{P} \in \mathbb{R}^n \,/\, \vec{P} \geq 0, \, y, \, \Sigma P_i = 1\}$$

being S a convex, closed and bounded set, then there is a price vector $\vec{P} \in S$ with function f: S → S such that:

$$E(\vec{P}) = \vec{P}^*$$

in other words, the demand surplus function has a Brower fixed point. The geometrical idea is very simple being S a defined set as a simple x S = [0, 1] which can be represented as a square of side 1:

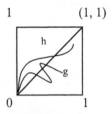

The Brower Theorem states that every continuous curve (g, h, ...: S → S) from left to right, must cross the diagonal at least once.

Therefore, a continuous (tâtonnement) function g: S → S must be made, which, under the Brower Theorem is:

$$g(\vec{P}) = \frac{P_i + k_i \max(0, E_i(\vec{P}))}{\Sigma_j P_j + \Sigma_j k_j \max(0, E_j(\vec{P}))}.$$

and, being now $k_i = 1, \forall_i$; since function:

g: $S \rightarrow S$

is continuos in $\vec{P}$, then function g: $S \rightarrow S$ has in fact S as domain and counter-domain and therefore, this function is well defined, continuous and is verified that:

$S = \{ \vec{P} \in \mathbb{R}^n / \vec{P} \geq 0, y, \Sigma P_i = 1 \}$

satisfies the Brower hypothesis. Thus, there is a vector $\vec{P}^*$ which is a fixed point of the "tâtonnement", in other words:

$g(\vec{P}^*) = \vec{P}^*$

Now we must demonstrate that $\vec{P}^* / E(\vec{P}^*) \leq 0$:

Each coordinate of vector $g(\vec{P}^*)$ is defined as:

$$P_i = \frac{P_i + \max(0, E_i(\vec{P}^*))}{\Sigma_j P_j^* + \Sigma_j \max(0, E_j(\vec{P}^*))}$$

multiplying by E and adding, we have that:

$$\Sigma P_i^* E_i(P^*) = \frac{\Sigma P_i^* E_i(P^*) + \Sigma E_i(\vec{P}^*) \max(0, E_i(\vec{P}^*))}{\Sigma P_i^* + \Sigma \max(0, E_j(\vec{P}^*))}$$

By applying Walras' Law:

$\Sigma E_i(\vec{P}^*) \max(0, E_i, (\vec{P}^*)) = 0$

therefore:

$$\Sigma P_i^* E_i(P^*) = \frac{\Sigma P_i^* E_i(\vec{P}^*) + 0}{\Sigma P_i^* + \Sigma \max(0, E_j(\vec{P}^*))}$$

If $E_i(\vec{P}) > 0$, then, the last statement becomes an addend of the addition of squares whose total addition is zero, and where each addend is higher than or equal to zero, which cannot occur. Thus:

$E(\vec{P}) \leq 0$

On the other hand, if constant returns to scale exist the producers' response may not be only one, which leads $E(\vec{P}^*)$ to be not well defined. The Kakutani Theorem solves this case. It associates to each $\vec{P}$ a set S and a function $E(\vec{P})$ which is semi-continuous on the top and which also gives conditions under which a fixed point is guaranteed.

1.4
The Third Stage of GE: Unicity and Stability

After the first two stages we have the Arrow-Debreu model (in the professional jargon) available, which presents a very desired property:

"The existence of equilibrium on the basis of very few fundamental hypotheses". However, it is easy to find several equilibriums (non-unicity) and, in this case, some of them may be unstable (non-stability).

1.4.1 The Walrasian GE Model Extended by Arrow-Debreu and Gale-Nikaido

In order to demonstrate the unicity of a GE model extended by Arrow-Debreu, now it is necessary to extend the model to satisfy Gale and the Nikaido Theorem. These authors use the supply surplus function rather than the demand surplus function, thus, $S(\vec{P})$ being defined as:

$$S(\vec{P}) = -E(\vec{P})$$

where $E(\vec{P})$ has already been defined as a demand surplus. The price vector $\vec{P} \geq 0$ will be an equilibrium vector if $S(\vec{P}) \geq 0$.

Moreover $S(\vec{P})$ will be regular if it satisfies the following conditions:

a) $S(\vec{P})$ is differentiable for standardized prices.
b) The n-th good with positive price is the *numerarie* one.

1.4.1.1 The Gale-Nikaido Unicity Theorem (Canonic Approach)

The Gale-Nikaido Unicity Theorem. If demand surplus $E(\vec{P})$ satisfies the degree-zero homogeneity and differentiability conditions as well as Walras' Law, being good n *numerarie*, then, there is a single equilibrium price vector provided that the square matrix of order n-1 of $S(\vec{P}) = (S_{ij}(\vec{P}))$ is a matrix where all the main minors are positive (a p-matrix).

1.4.1.2 Demonstration (Canonic Approach: Gale-Nikaido)

Demonstration of Unicity:

Since $S(\vec{P})$ is degree-zero homogeneous, by the Euler theorem:

$$\sum_{i \neq n} S_{ij}(\vec{P})P_i + S_{in}(\vec{P}) = 0; \ \forall i = 1, ..., n-1$$

in other words:

$$\sum_{i \neq n} S_{ij}(\vec{P})P_i = -S_{in}(\vec{P})$$

where

$$-S_{in}(\vec{P}) = E_{in}(\vec{P}); \ \forall i \neq n$$

and where

$$S_{ij}(\vec{P}) = -E_{ij}(\vec{P}); \ \forall i, j = 1, ..., n-1$$

n-1 order square matrix.

$$-E_{ij}(\vec{P}) \cdot \vec{P} = a$$

This equation system satisfies Hawkins-Simon's conditions: S is a matrix with diagonal non-positive elements. Given that a ≥ 0, vector $\vec{P} \geq 0$ is the solution to the equation system, which is equivalent to the fact that S is a matrix (p-matrix) where all main minors are positive.

The above unicity theorem lacks clarity from an economic point of view since it considers a square matrix of order n-1 which is a p-matrix. However, the notion of p-matrix is equivalent to the fact that the main minors are positive, in other words:

$$S_{ij}(\vec{P}) = \partial S_i / \partial P_j > 0; \; \partial E(\vec{P}) / \partial P_j < 0; \; \forall i \neq j$$

Or simply that the gross substitutability condition is satisfied:

$$\partial x_i / \partial P_j > 0; \; x_i \text{ gross substitute of } x_j.$$

Then, it is possible to reformulate the Gale-Nikaido Theorem as follows:

Reformulated the Gale-Nikaido Unicity Theorem. If demand surplus $E(\vec{P})$ satisfies degree-zero homogeneity and differentiability conditions as well as Walras' Law, being good n *numerarie*, then, there exists a single equilibrium price vector if gross substitutability condition is satisfied between the goods.

In a simple and easy way to remember:

The Unicity Theorem: If gross substitutability condition is satisfied, then, equilibrium is unique.

It is also possible to get this result with the revealed preference theory approach.

1.4.1.3 The Unicity Theorem (Revealed Preference Approach)

If the Weak Axiom of Revealed Preference is satisfied at the aggregate level, equilibrium is unique.

1.4.1.4 Demonstration (Revealed Preference Approach)

Demonstration of Unicity from the WARP.

$$\sum_{i=1}^{n} \vec{P}_i^* E_i(\vec{P}^*) \geq \sum_{i=1}^{n} \vec{P}_i^* E_i(\vec{P}) \Rightarrow \sum_{i=1}^{n} \vec{P}_i E_i(\vec{P}^*) > \sum_{i=1}^{n} \vec{P}_i E_i(\vec{P})$$

Assume that there are two equilibrium vectors:

$$\vec{P}^* \text{ y } \vec{P}, \text{ where } \vec{P}^* \neq \vec{P}$$

if $\vec{P}$ is the equilibrium vector, then:

$$\Sigma_i \vec{P}_i^* E_i(\vec{P}^*) \geq \Sigma_i \vec{P}_i^* E_i(\vec{P}) \Rightarrow \Sigma_i \vec{P}_i E_i(\vec{P}^*) > \Sigma_i \vec{P}_i E_i(\vec{P})$$

Likewise, if $\vec{p}_i^*$ is the equilibrium price vector:

$$\Sigma_i \vec{P}_i E_i(\vec{P}) \geq \Sigma_i \vec{P}_i E_i(\vec{P}^*) \Rightarrow \Sigma_i \vec{P}_i^* E_i(\vec{P}) > \Sigma_i \vec{P}_i^* E_i(\vec{P}^*)$$

therefore:

$$\Sigma_i \vec{P}_i^* E_i(\vec{P}^*) < \Sigma_i \vec{P}_i^* E_i(\vec{P}) \leq \Sigma_i \vec{P}_i^* E_i(\vec{P}^*)$$

then:

$$\Sigma_i \vec{P}_i^* \, E_i(\vec{P}^*) < \Sigma_i \vec{P}_i^* \, E_i(\vec{P}^*)$$

which represents an inconsistency so there is only one equilibrium price vector. c.q.d.

1.4.1.5 Proposition of Perfect Static Stability

In order to guarantee equilibrium stability it is required that the GE is satisfied with Arrow-Debreu and Gale-Nikaido's modifications under the notions of Hicks' static stability and local and global dynamics. Therefore, there are different concepts of stability. First, we have Hicks' perfect stability (HPS)

Proposition 1:
The market of a particular good x_i presents Hicks' perfect stability (HPS, also called perfect static stability) if, as the price of the good goes down, its demand is higher than supply, in other words:

$$d \, E_i(\vec{p}) / d \, P_i < 0$$

and this adjustment in i does not unsettle other markets already in equilibrium.

Hicks demonstrated that this concept of stability is equivalent to the fact that the main minors of the Jacobian matrix of n-1 demand surpluses,

$$J_{ij} = \partial \, E_i(\vec{p}) / \partial \, P_j; \; \forall i, j = 1, 2, ..., n\text{-}1$$

alternate in signs. In other words, if the main minors satisfy the rule of sign $|J_{ij}|$ $(-1)^i > 0$, then, all the system markets have HPS.

1.4.1.6 The Perfect Static Stability Theorem (Canonic Approach: Hicks)

The HPS theorem. If the Jacobian matrix of n-1 functions of demand surplus is such that its main minors satisfy $|J_{ij}| \, (-1)^i > 0$ all the system markets have HPS.

1.4.1.7 Demonstration (Canonic Approach)

The Static Stability Theorem or the Hicks Theorem. The Jacobian matrix of n-1 demand surpluses.

$$\partial \, E_i(\vec{p}) / \partial \, \vec{p}_j \; ; (\forall i, j = 1, 2, ..., n\text{-}1)$$

is perfectly stable if its main minors alternate in sign starting with negative. In other words, being M the main minors: $(-1)^i \, M_i > 0$.

Demonstration

On the whole, the equation system, by the rule of chain is:

$$\partial \, E_i(\vec{p}) / \partial \, \vec{p}_j = \sum_{k=1}^{n-1} \frac{\partial E_i(\vec{P})}{\partial \vec{P}_k} \frac{\partial P_k}{\partial P_j} \; ; \text{with } P_k = P_k (P_1, ..., P_n)$$

If we adjust P_1 by fixing all the other equations, then

$\partial E_1(\bar{P}) / \partial \bar{P}_1 = E_{11} < 0$

Analogously,

$\partial E_i(\bar{P}) / \partial \bar{P}_i = E_{ii} < 0$

If P_1 already has equilibrium, then we adjust P_2:

$0 = dE_1(\bar{P}) / d\bar{P}_1 = E_{11} + E_{12}(dP_2/dP_1)$

$\partial E_2(\bar{P}) / \partial \bar{P}_2 = E_{21}(dP_1/dP_2) + E_{22}$

$\partial E_2(\bar{P}) / \partial \bar{P}_2 = E_{21} - E_{12}/E_{11} + E_{22} = (E_{22}E_{11} - E_{21}E_{12})/E_{11} < 0$

Since $E_{11} < 0$, it is required that:

$E_{22}E_{11} - E_{21}E_{12} > 0$

$$(-1)^2 M_2 = \begin{vmatrix} E_{11} & E_{12} \\ E_{21} & E_{22} \end{vmatrix} = E_{11}E_{22} - E_{21}E_{12} > 0$$

then, in the next stage we will have:

$$(-1)^3 M_3 = \begin{vmatrix} E_{11} & E_{12} & E_{13} \\ E_{21} & E_{22} & E_{23} \\ E_{31} & E_{32} & E_{33} \end{vmatrix} > 0$$

and so on we will have $(-1)^i M_i > 0$.

1.4.1.8 The Local Dynamic Stability (Canonic Approach)

Hicks also demonstrated that the only source of instability in general competitive equilibrium is the asymmetry of the income effects, in other words:

The reviewed HPS theorem. If the return effects of all consumers are symmetric, then, a competitive economy presents HPS. (Demonstration in Quirk and Saposnik (1968)).

The concept of HPS stability or static stability we have dealt with so far does not assign any relevant role to time, therefore it is necessary to introduce the notion of dynamic stability (DS).

A dynamic system of prices such as $\dot{P} = \psi(E(\bar{P}))$ is dynamically stable if price vector $\bar{P}$ and equilibrium prices $\bar{P}^*$ ($t \to \infty$) converge; where $\dot{P} = d\bar{P}_i/dt$; ψ_i is the speed of adjustment, being an increasing function such that $\psi_i(0) = 0$.

Now, we will distinguish between local and global dynamic stable equilibrium. Equilibrium presents local dynamic stability (LDS) when its small disturbances result in an automatic return to the initial equilibrium. Equilibrium presents global dynamic stability (GDS) when, after considering as many big deviations or disturbances as we desire, initial equilibrium is automatically achieved.

1.4.1.9 The Local Dynamic Stability Theorem (Canonic Approach)

The LDS Theorem. If all the goods of an economy are gross substitutes between one another that economy presents local dynamic stability (LDS).

1.4.1.10 Demonstration (Canonic Approach)

The Local Dynamic Stability Theorem: If all the goods are gross substitutes equilibrium has local dynamic stability.

Demonstration

Being $\vec{P}_r$ a price vector such that it makes that:

$$\vec{P}\,E(\vec{P}) = 0$$

we derive this statement with respect to $\vec{P}_r$ and we have that:

$$\sum_{j=1}^{n} P_j \frac{\partial E(\vec{P})}{\partial \vec{P}_r} + E_r$$

Being now P* the only equilibrium price vector, then:

$$\sum_{j=1}^{n} P_j^* \left[\frac{\partial E(\vec{P})}{\partial P_r} \right]_{P^*} = 0$$

Now we take the first term of the addend and place it on the left, that is to say:

$$\sum_{j=2}^{n} P_j^* \frac{\partial E_j}{\partial P_r} = -P_1^* \frac{\partial E_1}{\partial P_r} = -\frac{\partial E_1}{\partial P_r}$$

Now we will obtain the derivative of the demand surplus function:

$$\sum_{j=2}^{n} P_j^* \frac{\partial E_j}{\partial P_r} < \frac{\partial E_r}{\partial P_r} P_r^*$$

$\{\partial E(\vec{P})/\partial P_r\}$ is a square matrix with negative main dominating diagonal since all the main diagonal roots are negative and all the remaining roots are positive.
If all the main diagonal roots are negative the own price effects are negative and, if the remaining roots are positive the goods are gross substitutes. Therefore, if the goods are gross substitutes, they present negative main diagonal and Local Dynamic Stability.

1.4.1.11 The Global Dynamic Stability Theorem (Canonic Approach)

The Global Dynamic Stability Theorem: If all the goods of an economy are gross substitutes between one another, their $E(\vec{P})$ functions are continuous degree-one homogeneous and satisfy Walras' Law, this economy presents global dynamic stability (GDS).

The theory of differential equations provides useful information in order to achieve global dynamic stability. This information is that, in those cases in which it is possible to make a Liapunov function the existence of global dynamic stability is guaranteed.

We will start from the system $\dot{\vec{P}} = E(\vec{P})$, $E(\vec{P})$ having degree-zero homogeneity and satisfying Walras' Law. Therefore, the concept of gross substitutability applied to the equilibrium point guarantees that it is possible to make a Liapunov function so the system is globally stable.

1.4.1.12 Demonstration (Canonic Approach)

The Global Dynamic Stability Theorem: If all the goods are gross substitute, the equilibrium is globally stable.

Here we will study the stability of $d\vec{P}/dt = E(\vec{P})$ under the homogeneity assumptios, Walras' Law and gross substitutability of the goods.

Being now that:

$$v(t) = \frac{1}{2} \sum_{i=1}^{n} (\vec{P}_i(t) - \vec{P}_i^*)^2$$

if this function satisfies that $v(t)$ reaches a minimum in $\vec{P}^*$ and that $dv(t)/dt < 0$, then it is a Liapunov function and is globally stable.

We make $\vec{P}^*$ such that:

$$\sum_{i=1}^{n} (\vec{P}_i^*)^2 = \sum_{i=1}^{n} \vec{P}_i^2(0)$$

thus we derive $v(t)$ with respect to time:

$$\frac{dv(t)}{dt} = \sum_{i=1}^{n} (\vec{P}_i - \vec{P}_i^*) \frac{d\vec{P}}{dt} = \sum_{i=1}^{n} (\vec{P}_i - \vec{P}_i^*) E(\vec{P})$$

and finally:

$$\frac{dv(t)}{dt} = \sum_{i=1}^{n} \frac{d\vec{P}_i}{dt} \vec{P}_i - \sum_{i=1}^{n} \frac{d\vec{P}_i^*}{dt} \vec{P}_i^*$$

$$\frac{dv(t)}{dt} = - \sum_{i=1}^{n} \vec{P}_i^* E(\vec{P}) < 0$$

Now, if $\vec{P}_i^* E(\vec{P}) > 0$ we can guarantee global stability.

$\vec{P}^*$ is the unique equilibrium vector since if $\vec{P} \neq \vec{P}^*$ then $\vec{P}^* E(\vec{P}) > 0$. The idea consists of the fact that function $\vec{P} \rightarrow \vec{P}^* E(\vec{P})$ has a minimum at $\vec{P}^*$ and is a continuous function evaluated in a compact set - since prices are standardized -. Thus, the minimum has to exist and function $\vec{P}^* E(\vec{P})$ has null derivative at the minimum. The concept of gross substitution (applied to the equilibrium point) gives a contradiction unless the minimum is precisely $\vec{P}^*$.

Considering now function:

$$g(t) = \sum_{i=1}^{n} \vec{P}_i^2(t)$$

if we derive it with respect to t and apply Walras' Law, we have that:

$$D\left[\sum_{i=1}^{n} \vec{P}_i^2(t)\right] = 2\sum_{i=1}^{n} \vec{P}_i(t)\,(d\vec{P}_i/dt) = 2\,\vec{p}\,E(\vec{p}) = 0$$

g (t) is a constant function, therefore:

$$\sum_{i=1}^{n} \vec{P}_i^2(t) = \sum_{i=1}^{n} \vec{P}_i^2(0)$$

$$v(t) = \tfrac{1}{2}\sum_{i=1}^{n} (\vec{P}_i(t) - \vec{P}_i^*)^2 < 0$$

where $\vec{p}^*$ is such that:

$$\sum_{i=1}^{n} \vec{P}_i^2(t) = \sum_{i=1}^{n} P_i^2(0)$$

thus:

$$\frac{dv(t)}{dt} = \sum_{i=1}^{n} (\vec{P}_i - \vec{P}_i^*)\frac{d\vec{P}}{dt} = \sum_{i=1}^{n} (\vec{P}_i - \vec{P}_i^*)\,E(\vec{p}) = -\sum_{i=1}^{n} \vec{P}_i^*\,E_i(\vec{p}) < 0.$$

And it is a Liapunov function indicating that there is global stability.

1.4.1.13 The Global Dynamic Stability Theorem (Revealed Preference Approach)

It is possible to prove GDS from the weak axiom of revealed preference WARP.

The reformulated GDS Theorem. If the functions of demand surplus $E(\vec{p})$ are continuous and degree-zero homogeneous and they satisfy Walras' Law and the WARP, the equilibrium presents GDS.

1.4.1.14 Demonstration (Revealed Preference Approach)

Can we guarantee that $\vec{P}_i^*\,E(\vec{p}) > 0$?

Under the Weak Axiom of Revealed Preference (WARP), we have that if:

$$\vec{p}\,E(\vec{p}) \geq \vec{p}\,E(\vec{p}^*) \;\Rightarrow\; \vec{p}^*E(\vec{p}^*) < P^*\,E(\vec{p})$$
$$\text{WARP}$$

by Walras' Law:

$$\vec{p}\,E(\vec{p}) = 0 \text{ and } \vec{p}^*E(\vec{p}^*) = 0$$

therefore:

$$0 \geq P\,E(P^*) \;\Rightarrow\; P^*\,E(P^*) < P^*\,E(P)$$
$$\text{WARP}$$

so $\vec{p}^*\,E(\vec{p}) > 0$.

Bibliographic References

Arrow, K.: Alternative Demonstration of ohe Substitution Theorem for Leontief Models in the General Case. En: Koopmans, T. (ed.), Activity Analysis of Production and Allocation. 155-64. New York: Wiley 1951

Arrow, K, Debreu, G.: Existence of Equilibrium for a Competitive Economy. Econometrica 22, 265-50 (1954)

Debreu, G: The Coefficient of Resonice Utilization. Econometrica 19/13, 273-292 (1951)

Debreu. G.: Game of Value. New York: Wiley 1959

Friedman, J.N.: Game Theory with Applications to Economics. Oxford University Press 1986

Hildenbrand, W., Kirman, A.: Introduction to Equilibrium Analysis. Amsterdam: North – Holland 1976

Quirck, J., Saposniv, R.: Introduction to General Equilibrium Theory and Welfare Economics. New York: McGraw Hill 1968

Smith, A.: An Inquiry into the Nature and Causes of the Wealth of Nations. 1776
   [Translated into Spanish as: Investigación sobre la Naturaleza y Causas de la Riqueza de las Naciones. Mexico: Fund of Economic Culture 1979]

Walras, L.: Eléments d'Economie Politique Rue où Theorie de la Richesse Sociale. Lausanne: Coba 7 1874
   [Translated into English as: Elements of Pure Economics. Homewood: Irwin 1954]

2 Other Models of General Equilibrium

In this chapter my aim is to develop some of the dynamic economic applications generated by non-linear systems.

Two models have been chosen: a classic growth model and a model of successive generations. The reason for this choice is to illustrate how both classic traditional and modern models such as those of successive generation serve to generate complex dynamics in spite of the deterministic character of them both.

The models used are quite simple. The main objective of this chapter is to offer straightforward models of general equilibrium with complex equilibrium results as regards existence, unicity and stability.

2.1
Model 1

This model is based on Baumol's version (1970). This version was studied and partly modified by Day (1983) with the aim of showing how fluctuations of an erratic and unstable nature can appear in the population. The previous version by Day has been slightly altered so that the model enables us to obtain a stationary solution as well as stable periodic results and chaotic results.

Below we offer an introduction to the application of the concept of complexity in an economy. However, two things may be surprising. First, the nature of the complex mathematics itself and secondly, the capacity of a non-linear model to generate unusually different results without any variation in the model.

2.1.1 Assumptions

i) We assume an economy with only one sector (agriculture) where the total product Y_t depends on the amount of working population P_t.

$Y_t = f(P_t)$, con $f'(P_t) > 0$ y $f''(P_t) < 0$

where $f'(P_t) > 0$ expresses the positive character of the marginal product of labor and where $f''(P_t) < 0$ indicates the existence of decreasing returns. We assume that $f(0) = 0$ and that the function is continuous and concave.

ii) We assume that the total product Y_t, is distributed according to the mean product. In other words, we assume that the wage is equal to the mean productivity.

$w_t = f(P_t)/P_t$

iii) We assume that the population growth rate in per capita terms is ruled by function:

$$\Delta P_t/P_t = \min [\lambda, (w-\sigma)/\sigma]$$

where $\Delta P/P$ is the population growth rate, λ is the maximum growth rate of population which enables the most advantageous biological conditions and $(w-\sigma)/\sigma$ is the maximum growth rate which permits the current availability of food, such availability culturally determined by the current wages. When wages are at a subsistence level $w = \sigma$ the rate is null and population remains stationary. The level of subsistence σ can be considered as determined by sociological or cultural factors.

2.1.2 Development of the Model

Under the previous assumptions, the function which rules the population growth is:

$$\Delta P/P = \min [\lambda, (w-\sigma)/\sigma] \tag{2.1}$$

Given this, if we substitute the statement in (2.1) we obtain:

$$(P_{t+1} - P_t) / P_t = \min [\lambda, (w-\sigma)/\sigma]$$

$$P_{t+1} / P_t = \min [(\lambda + 1); w/\sigma]$$

$$P_{t+1} = \min [(\lambda + 1) P_t; (w/\sigma) P_t] \tag{2.2}$$

this equation describes the evolution of a sequence of generations. Under ii) assumption we can substitute in (2.2) and obtain:

$$P_{t+1} = \min [(\lambda + 1) P_t; f (P_t)/\sigma)] \tag{2.3}$$

This equation shows that the population growth is determined by two regimes. Under the first regime the population growth rate is controlled by biological rate λ while under the second regime it is controlled by the maximum rate with level of subsistence σ. These two population growth rates give rise to what we call two phases of population: biological and subsistence.

2.1.3 The Solution

Two possible results of the model are:

a) The stationary solution.
b) Stable cycles of different periods.
c) Chaotic results.

The stationary solution of the classic growth model will always have subsistence wages. With wages higher than the level of subsistence, population grows continuously and wages also fall in a continuous way.

On the other hand, with wages below the level of subsistence, population decreases since $(w-\sigma)/\sigma$ is a negative number and therefore, it results lower than λ.

In other words, with wages below the level of subsistence, population continuously decreases, which leads to an increase in wages. Therefore, wages different from those of the level of subsistence cannot be considered in equilibrium.

Let's see now what happens with $w = \sigma$ (that is to say, when wages are initially at the level of subsistence). Given that wages are assumed equal to the mean product, it must be verified that $f(P_t) / P_t = \sigma$. This statement is an equation with only one unknown quantity: P_t. Value P_t, which satisfies equation P_e, can be considered as the stationary equilibrium population. Therefore, when $P_t = P_e$, wage is at the level of subsistence and population remains constant over each period.

For levels of population below P_e, wages will be higher than the level of subsistence and population will grow up to P_e at natural rate λ during the first period and at rate $(w-\sigma)/\sigma$ during the second period. There will be a monotonous population growth in the phase of subsistence up to the level of equilibrium population. This process is represented in figure 2.1.

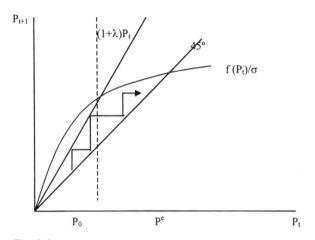

Fig. 2.1

As observed in the graphs, as long as $f(P_t)$ increases and becomes concave the stationary solution represents the only stable solution of the system (figure 2.1). However, this is not given when $f(P_t)$ has a decreasing branch (at a certain point, a surplus population is produced and workers block one another so the total output starts falling). In this case the stationary solution may be stable (a case illustrated in figure 2.2) but it may not be, as happens in figures 2.3 and 2.4. In these last cases there are more or less complex cycles which are repeated regularly.

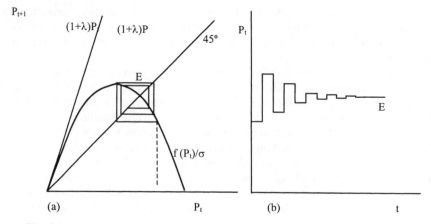

Fig. 2.2

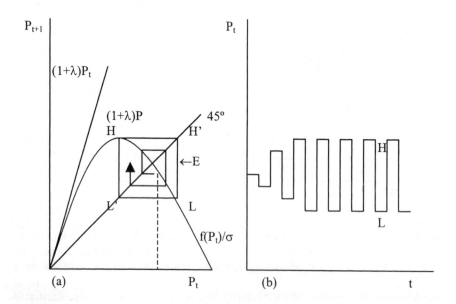

Fig. 2.3

"Chaotic" solutions are also possible, as occurs in figures 2.5, 2.6 and 2.7. This means that periods of abundance and scarcity (periods with rapidly increasing population and periods with decreasing population) may alternate without any order and in apparent "chaos".

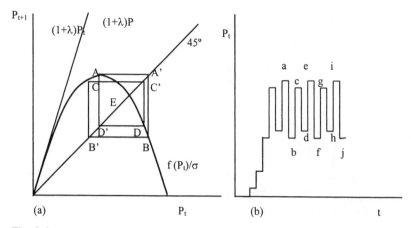

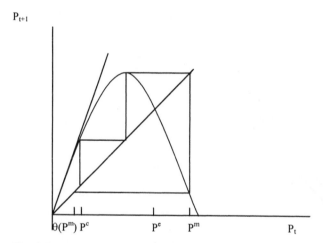

Fig. 2.4

Fig. 2.5

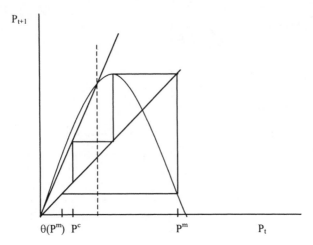

$\theta(P^m)$ P^c P^m P_t

Fig. 2.6

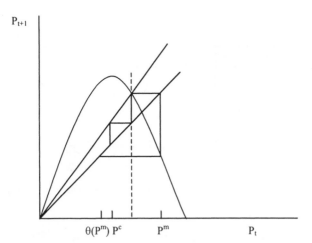

$\theta(P^m)$ P^c P^m P_t

Fig. 2.7

How can we know that there is chaos in these cases? We know this through the Li-Yorke theorem enunciated below.

2.1.4 The Li-Yorke Theorem (Baumol and Benhabid's Version, 1989)

Assume that we have a continuous function in differences of the type $P_{t+1}=f(P_t)$ and that there is some interval (a,b) such that the whole cycle initiated within said interval never exceeds the limits. If this assumption, - which does not seem restrictive and in which $P_3 < P_o < P_1 < P_2$ - is satisfied, we can state the following:

1. For any whole number $k > 1$ we can find at least one initial condition (in other words, a value Po) which generates cycles of period k. This implies that there are virtually infinite cyclic-possibilities which do not lead to equilibrium.
2. Within interval (a,b) there is a disordered and uncountable set of points such that any pair of initial curves within said set may become infinitely close together at any point to later separate from each other but they never converge between themselves or with any other type of regular or periodic curve.

In the growth model we are analyzing the above theorem is satisfied as can be appreciated in figures 2.5, 2.6 and 2.7.

2.2
Model 2

The model here presented is based on the work by Diamond (1965) and is used together with Benhabid and Day's further version (1980 and 1982).

2.2.1 Assumptions of the Model

i) Assume that individuals live two time periods t and t+1 at a time t and two generations exist at the same time: 0 and 1. Only young people work, who save part of their income and are actually the ones who acquire capital stock with their savings. The capital stock available for the individual who invests during the period t+1 is called k_{t+1} and equals the capital stocks saved by the subject during period t.

$$k_{t+1} = w_t - c_0(t)$$

In the above statement, w_t is the wage and c_o (t) is the individual's consumption born in generation 0 during period t. We also assume that the capital stock of each period is wholly consumed within that period. This implies that the capital stock available during t+1 equals that invested in period t.

$$I_t = k_{t+1}$$

ii) Assuming that an individual who represents the younger generation only receives income from work, this individual earns a wage w which he must distribute in the two periods of his life t and t+1. This means that his consumption during period t+1 will be given by the following statement:

$$c_0(t+1) = [w_t - c_0(t)] \cdot (1 + r_{t+1})$$

where r_{t+1} is the interest rate of savings from period t to t+1. In other words, the economic agent can save and, through the credit market, transfer resources from the first period of life to the second.

iii) Assume that the population of both generations remains always the same.

iv) Assume that the utility function for each generation is of the Cobb-Douglas type and is given by:

$$u_t = c_0(t)^\beta \cdot c_0(t+1)^{(1-\beta)}$$

or in logarithmic form:

$$\text{Ln } u_t = \beta \text{ Ln } c_0(t) + (1 - \beta) \text{ Ln } c_0(t+1)$$

Here β is a parameter which measures the subject's availability in order to replace present consumption with future consumption. The higher β is the higher the marginal rate of substitution between present and future consumption will be (in other words, the $dc_0(t+1)/dc_0(t)$ ratio in absolute value). It is assumed that β increases as wage increases. That is to say:

$$\beta = \beta(w) = a \cdot w_t$$

being $a > 0$.
v) Assume that individual production function is of the Cobb-Douglas type:

$$f(k_t) = A \cdot k_t^\alpha.$$

2.2.2 Development of the Model

2.2.2.1 Individuals' Behavior: Inter-temporal Maximization

The individuals who represents the initial generation 0 in period t will maximize their utility function given a level of wages and an market interest rate and they will assign their consumption in such a way that:

$$\frac{\partial u_t / \partial c_0(t)}{\partial u_t / \partial c_0(t+1)} = (1 + r_{t+1})$$

$$c_0(t+1) = [w_t - c_0(t)] \cdot (1 + r_{t+1})$$

$$c_0(t) = \theta (w_t, r_{t+1})$$

$$c_0(t+1) = \psi (w_t, r_{t+1})$$

From above we derive that:

$$w_t - \theta (w_t, r_{t+1}) = s_t$$

$$s_t = s (w_t, r_{t+1})$$

Therefore, the saved amount may be expressed as a function of the relevant levels of wage and interest:

$$s_t = s (w_t, r_{t+1}); \ 0 < s_w < 1; \ s_r \text{ indeterminate}$$

If s is a differentiable function, the normality assumption gives us the direction of the partial derivative with respect to w. However, the sign of the partial derivative with respect to r may be either positive or negative depending on the intensity of the substitution and income effects. The substitution effect always has positive sign (an increase in r leads to an increase in saving: future consumption is encouraged at the expense of present consumption) and the income effect has negative sign (an increase in r leads to an increase in present and future consumption so saving decreases). In fact, a high increase in consumption may take place in the first and second period when the individuals' wages increase sufficiently.

Companies hire work and capital in perfect competition, therefore, it will be verified that the respective marginal productivity will fix the prices of capital and wages.

$$f'(k_t) = r_t$$

$$f'(k_t) - k_t \cdot f'(k_t) = w_t$$

where k_t is the capital-labor ratio of companies.

Equilibrium in goods market requires that the demand for goods equals supply within the same period. This implies that saving must equal investment in aggregate terms and the fact that all the accumulation of k comes from youngsters means that savings per young individual must equal investment per young individual. That is to say:

$$k_{t+1} = s\,[(w_t, (1 + r_{t+1})]$$

In other words, older individuals "consume" the capital stock of the previous period.

Since labor services are fixed $L = L_o$, labor supply is perfectly inelastic. The capital supply in period t+1 is determined according to the saving decisions made in period t. Equilibrium in the input market also requires that the wage rate and the capital interest ratio of firms equal the respective marginal products.

2.2.2.2 Equilibrium Dynamics and State

Utility maximization subjected to budget restriction implies that:

$$\frac{\partial u_t / \partial c_0(t)}{\partial u_t / \partial c_0(t+1)} = (1 + r_{t+1})$$

$$\partial u_t / \partial c_0(t) = \beta / c_0(t)$$

$$\partial u_t / \partial c_0(t+1) = (1 - \beta) / c_0(t+1)$$

Then:

$$\frac{\beta / c_0(t)}{(1-\beta) / c_0(t+1)} = (1 + r_{t+1})$$

By assumption ii):

$$c_0(t+1) = [w_t - c_0(t)] \cdot (1 + r_{t+1})$$

By substituting:

$$\frac{\beta / c_0(t)}{(1-\beta)/[w_t - c_0(t)] \cdot (1 + r_{t+1})} = (1 + r_{t+1})$$

$$\beta / (1 - \beta) = c_0(t) / [w_t - c_0(t)] = (w_t - k_{t+1}) / k_{t+1}$$

$$\beta \cdot k_{t+1} = (1 - \beta) \cdot (w_t - k_{t+1})$$

$$\beta \cdot k_{t+1} = w_t - k_{t+1} - \beta \cdot w_t + \beta \cdot k_{t+1}$$

$$k_{t+1} = w_t \cdot (1 - \beta)$$

Given the assumption that $\beta = a \cdot w_t$ we can write:

$$k_{t+1} = w_t \, (1 - a \, w_t) \tag{2.4}$$

By substituting the equilibrium conditions in the input market and the definition of each production function:

$$k_{t+1} = A \cdot k_t^\alpha \cdot (1 - \alpha) \cdot [1 - a \cdot A \cdot k_t^\alpha \cdot (1 - \alpha)]$$

2.2.3 The Solution

The above equation has a single and stable solution as long as:

$$\left| \frac{dk_{t+1}}{dk_t} \right| < 1$$

How can we know whether this is satisfied?
  By estimating:

$$\frac{dk_{t+1}}{dk_t} = \alpha A k_t^{\alpha-1}(1-\alpha) - a2\alpha A^2 k_t^{2\alpha-1}(1-\alpha)^2$$

We ignore whether the absolute value of this derivative is higher, lower than or equal to 1. This will depend on the values of A, a and α. Nothing can be ensured without more restrictions about the course of the accumulated capital stock. However, we can guarantee that chaotic dynamics can appear in the model for certain values of A, a and α since Li-York's sufficient condition is satisfied. For example, for A = 80, a = 1 and α = 0,95, with K_0 = 0,0384 we obtain from equation (2.4) the following values:

$K_1 = 0,148105$

$K_2 = 0,2269627$

$K_3 = 0,0217787$

Therefore:

$K_3 < K_0 < K_1 < K_2$

Then, Li-York's sufficient condition is verified.

Graphically, we will have equilibrium state when:

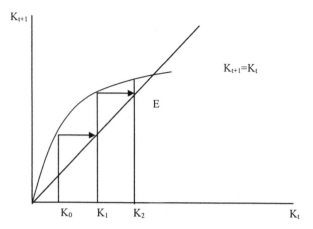

Fig. 2.8.

And, by analogy with model 1, figure 2.1, we can make from this model similar figures to those obtained in Figures 2.2 - 2.7.

2.3
Final Remarks

Two conclusions are reached from the above analysis taking into account the restrictions of the initial hypotheses:

First; the significant changes produced in the behavior of an economy do not prevent us from understanding how it works. In spite of the fact that the economy may be as unpredictable as the weather, we can still understand how it operates.

Second; the existence of complex dynamics gives rise to many doubts about predictions in economy.

This type of analysis is still at its initial stage. Virtually no empirical applications of it exist. However, I think that this analysis may result useful to study some phenomenon such as the economic cycles.

It seems that considerable economic literature in this field has been developed in recent years, a summary of which is offered below.

Bibliographic References

Arrow, K.J., McManus, M.: A Note on Dynamic Stability. Econométrica 26, 448-454 (1958)

Azariadis, C., Guesnerie, R.: Sunspost and Cycles. Review of Economic Studies 53, 725-737 (1986)

Baumol, W.J.: Economic Dynamics. 3rd ed. The MacMillan Co, London 1970

Baumol, W.J.: Unpredictibiliy, Pseudorandomnes and Military: Civilian Budget Interactions. Revista Internazionale di Scienze Economiche e Commerciale XXXIII-4, 297-318 (1986)

Baumol, W.J., Benhabib, J.: Chaos: Significance, Mechanism, and Economic Applications. Journal of Economic Perspectives, 77-105 (1989)

Benhabib, J., Nishimura, K.: The Hopf Bifurcation and the Existence and Stability of Closed Orbits in Multisector Models of Optimal Economic Growth. Journal of Economic Theory 2, 421-444 (1979)

Benhabib, J., Day, R.H.: Erratic Accumulation. Economics Letters, 113-117 (1980)

Benhabib, J., Day, R.H.: Rational Choice and Erratic Behaviour. Review of Economic Theory 21, 459-471 (1981)

Benhabib, J., Day, R.H.: A Characterization of Erratic Dynamics in the Overlapping Generation Model. Journal of Economic Dynamics and Control, 37-55 (1982)

Benhabib, J., Miyao, T.: Some New Results on the Dynamics of the Dynamics of the Generalized Tobin Model. International Economic Review 22, 589-596 (1981)

Benhabib, J., Nishimura, K.: Stability of Equilibrium in Dynamic Models of Capital Theory. International Economic Review 22, 275-293 (1981)

Benhabib, J., Nishimura, K.: Competitive Equilibrium Cycles. Journal of Economic Theory 35, 284-306 (1985)

Blanchard, O.J.: Dynamic Effects of a Shift in Savings: The role of firms. Econométrica 51, 1583-1592 (1983)

Boldrin, M., Montrucchio, L.: On the Indeterminancy of Capital Accumulation Paths. Journal of Economy Theory 40, 26-39 (1986)

Boldrin, M.: Economías Dinámicas. Cuadernos Económicos de ICE 46-47 (1991)

Brock, W.A.: Distiguishing Ramdon and Deterministic Systems: Abridged Version. Journal of Economic Theory 40, 168-195 (1986)

Brock, W.A., Sayers, C.: Is the Business Cycle Characterized by Deterministic Chaos?. Journal of Monetary Economics 21, 71-90 (1988)

Brock, W.A., Malliaris, A.G.: Differential Equations, Stability and Chaos in Dynamic Economics. North Holland, Amsterdam 1989

Cass, D., Shell, K.: Introduction to Hamiltonian Dynamics in Economics. Journal of Economic Theory 12, 1-10 (1976)

Day, R.H.: Irregular Growth Cycles. American Economic Review 72, 406-414 (1982)

Day, R.H.: The Emergence of Chaos from Classic Economic Growth. Quarterly Journal of Economics 98, 201-213 (1983)

Deneckere, R.L., Pelikan, S.: Competitive Chaos. Journal of Economic Theory 40, 13-25 (1986)

Devaney, R.L.: An Introduction to Chaotic Dynamical System. Benjamin/Cunmings Publishing Company, Reading Massachusetts 1986

Gale, D.: Pure Exchange Equilibrium of Dynamic Economic Nobel. Journal of Economic Theory 6, 12-36 (1973)

Li, T., York, J.: Period Three Implies Chaos. American Mathematical Monthly 82, 985-992 (1975)

Santos, M.S., Bona, J.L.: On the Structure of the Equilibrium Price Set of Overlapping Generations Economies. Journal of Mathematical Economies 18, 209-231 (1989)

Santos, M.S.: Sobre la Programación Dinámica en Modelos Económicos. Revista Española de Economía 9, 7-29 (1992)

Stutzer, M.: Chaotic Dynamics and Bifurcation in Macro Model. Journal of Economic Dynamics and Control 2, 353-376 (1980)

3 General Equilibrium and Main Functional Forms of Utility and Production

3.1
The Pure Exchange Model for Cobb-Douglas Utility Function

Being an economy with two consumers with equal initial assignments of x and y, equal parameters α and $1-\alpha$, one of them with a Cobb-Douglas utility function:

$$U(x, y) = x^\alpha y^{1-\alpha}$$

where x, y are the goods which exist in the economy. Goods (x, y) are not produced but they are amounts of initial assignments - assumed as equal – for each one of the two consumers. Each individual will have an income R depending on the amount of goods (x, y) he can exchange. Thus, income R:

$$R = P_x x + P_y y$$

where $P_x x + P_y y$ are the prices of goods x and y respectively and they are considered as determined by the market in perfect competition conditions.

Each consumer's problem will be:

$$\text{max. } U(x, y) = x^\alpha y^{1-\alpha}$$

$$\text{s.to: } R = P_x x + P_y y$$

From the first order conditions of this problem we obtain the Marsahallian demands of x and y:

$$\left. \begin{array}{l} x = x\,(R, P_x, P_y); \ x = \alpha R/P_x \\ y = y\,(R, P_x, P_y); \ y = (1-\alpha)R/P_y \end{array} \right\} \quad \left. \begin{array}{l} x^D = \alpha R/P_x \\ y^D = (1-\alpha)R/P_y \end{array} \right\}$$

The quantities offered are the addition of the amounts owned by both individuals:

$$\overline{x}_A + \overline{x}_B = \overline{x}^S$$

$$\overline{y}_A + \overline{y}_B = \overline{y}^S$$

The general equilibrium situation may be now described as:

$$x^D = x^S \left.\right\}$$
$$y^D = y^S \left.\right\}$$

$$2\alpha R/P_x = \overline{x}^S \Rightarrow E(P_x) = 2\alpha R/P_x - \overline{x}^S$$

$$2(1-\alpha)R/P_y = \overline{y}^S \Rightarrow E(P_y) = 2(1-\alpha)R/P_y - \overline{y}^S$$

where $E(P_x)$ and $E(P_y)$ represent the respective demand surpluses which, in perfect competition conditions, will be null for goods x and y. This means that it is possible to determine equilibrium prices P_x, P_y such as:

$$P_x = 2\alpha R/\overline{x}^S$$

$$P_y = 2(1-\alpha)R/\overline{y}^S$$

Therefore, there are two positive equilibrium prices P_x, P_y for the pure exchange general equilibrium system.

Moreover, it is satisfied that:

$$\frac{P_x}{P_y} = \frac{MU_x^A}{MU_y^A} = \frac{\alpha x^{\alpha-1}y^{1-\alpha}}{x^{\alpha-1}(1-\alpha)y^{1-\alpha-1}} = MRS_{x,y}^A = MRS_{x,y}^B = \frac{MU_x^B}{MU_y^B}$$

and also that:

$$\frac{P_x}{P_y} = \frac{\alpha/\overline{x}^S}{(1-\alpha)/\overline{y}^S} = \frac{\alpha\overline{y}^S}{(1-\alpha)\overline{x}^S}$$

from which:

$$\frac{\overline{y}^S}{\overline{x}^S} = \frac{x^{\alpha-1}y^{1-\alpha}}{x^{\alpha}y^{1-\alpha-1}} = x^{\alpha-1-\alpha}y^{1-\alpha-1+\alpha+1} = \frac{y}{x}$$

then:

$$\frac{\overline{y}^S}{\overline{x}^S} = \frac{y}{x}.$$

3.2
The Pure Exchange Model for Two Agents with Cobb-Douglas Utility Functions and Constant Returns to Scale in Consumption, Different Initial Assignments of (x, y) and Distinct Parameters in Consumption (α, β)

Being an economy with two consumers A and B, one of them having a Cobb-Douglas utility function of the type:

$$U(x, y) = x^\alpha y^{1-\alpha}$$

where (x, y) are the two goods which exist in the economy and such goods are initial assignments (x^*_A, y^*_A) for individual A and (x^*_B, y^*_B) for individual B. Each individual has an income R_A and R_B and therefore, the problem for individual A is:

$$\text{max. } U_A(x_A, y_A) = \alpha_A{}^\alpha y_A{}^{1-\alpha} \Big\}$$

$$\text{s. to: } R_A = P_x \overline{x}_A + P_y \overline{y}_A$$

and for individual B it will be:

$$\text{max. } U_B(x_B, y_B) = \alpha_B{}^\beta y_B{}^{1-\beta} \Big\}$$

$$\text{s. to: } R_B = P_x \overline{x}_B + P_y \overline{y}_B$$

from the first order conditions we obtain the following Marshallian demands:

$$
\left.
\begin{aligned}
x_A &= \alpha \frac{R_A}{P_x} \\[2mm]
y_A &= (1-\alpha)\frac{R_A}{P_y}
\end{aligned}
\right\}
$$

$$
\left.
\begin{aligned}
x_B &= \beta\frac{R_B}{P_x} \\[2mm]
y_B &= (1-\beta)\frac{R_B}{P_y}
\end{aligned}
\right\}
$$

where α and β are the utility function parameters of consumers A and B.

The quantities offered are the addition of the amounts owned by both individuals:

$$
\left.
\begin{aligned}
\overline{x}_B + \overline{x}_A &= \overline{x}^S \\[2mm]
\overline{y}_B + \overline{y}_A &= \overline{y}^S
\end{aligned}
\right\}
$$

The general equilibrium situation will be now:

$$x^D = \overline{x}^S$$

$$y^D = \overline{y}^S$$

Therefore:

$$x_A + x_B = \alpha \frac{R_A}{P_x} + \beta\frac{R_B}{P_x} = \overline{x}^S \Rightarrow E(P_x) = \frac{1}{P_x}(\alpha R_A + \beta R_B) - \overline{x}^S$$

$$y_A + y_B = (1-\alpha)\frac{R_A}{P_y} + (1-\beta)\frac{R_B}{P_y} = \overline{y}^S \Rightarrow E(P_y) = \frac{1}{P_y}((1-\alpha)R_A + (1-\beta)R_B) - \overline{y}^S$$

where $E(P_x)$ and $E(P_y)$ represent the respective demand surpluses, which, in perfect competition conditions, will be null for goods x and y, thus being possible to find P_x and P_y as follows:

$$
\left.
\begin{aligned}
P_x &= \frac{\alpha R_A + \beta R_B}{\overline{x}^S} \\[2ex]
P_y &= \frac{(1-\alpha)R_A + (1-\beta)R_B}{\overline{x}^S}
\end{aligned}
\right\}
$$

where P_x and P_y are equilibrium prices for the pure exchange general equilibrium system.

3.3
The Pure Exchange Model with Cobb-Douglas Utility Functions, Returns to Scale and a Price for One Good as *Numerarie*

This model is very similar to the one above. Once the Marshallian demands have been obtained, their values are substituted in the following surplus demand function for good x:

$$
E_x(p_x, p_y) = (x_A - \overline{x}_A) + (x_B - \overline{x}_B)
$$

in other words:

$$
E_x(p_x, p_y) = \left(\alpha \frac{R_A}{P_x} - \overline{x}_A \right) + \left(\beta \frac{R_B}{P_x} - \overline{x}_B \right)
$$

In the statement above, it is again possible to replace R_A and R_B with their respective values, thus obtaining:

$$
E_x(p_x, p_y) = \left(\alpha \frac{p_x \overline{x}_A + p_y \overline{y}_B}{p_x} - \overline{x}_A \right) + \left(\beta \frac{p_x \overline{x}_B + p_y \overline{y}_B}{p_x} - \overline{x}_B \right)
$$

and, on the other hand:

$$
E_y(p_x, p_y) = \left((1-\alpha) \frac{R_A}{P_y} - \overline{y}_A \right) + \left((1-\beta) \frac{R_B}{P_y} - \overline{y}_B \right)
$$

$$
E_y(p_x, p_y) = \left((1-\alpha) \frac{p_x \overline{x}_A + p_y \overline{y}_A}{p_y} - \overline{y}_A \right) + \left((1-\beta) \frac{p_x \overline{x}_B + p_y \overline{y}_B}{p_y} - \overline{y}_B \right)
$$

Now, we can choose one of the prices (P_x, P_y) as *numerarie* so, in this case, the demand surplus functions will vary. Thus, if we choose y as *numerarie* so that the demand surplus functions are:

$$E_x(p_x,1) = \left(\alpha \frac{p_x\bar{x}_A + \bar{y}_A}{p_x} - \bar{x}_A\right) + \left(\beta \frac{p_x\bar{x}_B + \bar{y}_B}{p_x} - \bar{x}_B\right)$$

$$E_y(p_x,1) = \left((1-\alpha)\frac{p_x\bar{x}_A + \bar{y}_A}{1} - \bar{x}_A\right) + \left((1-\beta)\frac{p_x\bar{x}_B + \bar{y}_B}{1} - \bar{y}_B\right)$$

then, we will have two functions ED_x and ED_y, whose dependent variable is the surplus of price P_x. Now, it is possible to find out the equilibrium price P_x in any of the two demand surplus functions since, by Walras' Law, both demand surpluses will be zero and both of them will give the same equilibrium price P_x, notwithstanding the demand surplus equation we may solve. The Walrasian corollary or the surplus equation principle allows us to ensure that whatever the equation in which P_x, is determined may be, the result will be the same:

$$P_x = \frac{\alpha\bar{y}_A + \beta\bar{y}_B}{(1-\alpha)\bar{x}_A + (1-\beta)\bar{x}_B}$$

If we want to obtain the equilibrium price of P_y, we must take x as *numerarie*, the two new demand surplus functions being defined:

$$E_x(1,p_y) = \left(\alpha \frac{\bar{x}_A + \bar{y}_A p_y}{1} - \bar{x}_A\right) + \left(\beta \frac{\bar{x}_B + p_y\bar{y}_B}{1} - \bar{x}_B\right)$$

$$E_y(1,p_y) = \left((1-\alpha)\frac{\bar{x}_A + p_y\bar{y}_A}{p_y} - \bar{x}_A\right) + \left((1-\beta)\frac{\bar{x}_B + p_y\bar{y}_B}{p_y} - \bar{y}_B\right)$$

which determines the equilibrium price of P_y.

3.4
The Pure Exchange Model for a Specific Utility Function

Assuming that individual A has an initial assignment of 78 units of x and none of y and that his utility function is:

$$U_A = xy + 2x + 5y$$

$$E_x^A = x - 78 \quad \rightarrow \text{Demand surplus of x}$$

$$E_y^A = y \qquad \rightarrow \text{Demand surplus of y}$$

Now, the following must be given:

$$\text{max.}U_A = xy + 2x + 5y$$

s. to: $p_x E_x^A + p_y E_y^A = 0$

$$E_x^A = x - 70$$

$$E_y^A = y$$

The Lagrangian is now:

$$L(E_x^A, E_y^A, \lambda) = (E_x^A + 78)E_y^A + 2(E_x^A + 78) + 5E_y^A - \lambda(p_x E_x^A + p_y E_y^A)$$

$$\left.\begin{array}{l} \dfrac{\partial L}{\partial E_x^A} = E_y^A + 2 - \lambda_{p_x} = 0 \\[3ex] \dfrac{\partial L}{\partial E_y^A} = E_x^A + 83 - \lambda_{p_y} = 0 \\[3ex] \dfrac{\partial L}{\partial \lambda} = -(p_x E_x^A + p_y E_y^A) = 0 \end{array}\right\}$$

$$\left.\begin{array}{l} E_x^A = \dfrac{p_y}{p_x} - 41{,}5 \\[3ex] E_y^A = 41{,}5\dfrac{p_x}{p_y} - 1 \end{array}\right\}$$

The demand surpluses of individual A are functions which depend on the prices of goods x and y and which also have the property of being degree-zero homogeneous in prices.

The budget equation of individual A is now:

$$p_x\left(\frac{p_y}{p_x} - 41{,}5\right) + p_y\left(41{,}5\frac{p_x}{p_y} - 1\right) = 0$$

The static comparative which enables the above equation is that an increase in p_x with respect to p_y will lead to a decrease in E_x and an increase in E_y.

If we assume now another individual B with the following utility function:

$$U_B = xy + 4x + 2y$$

and has an initial assignment of 164 units of y and none of x, which allows us to express the demand surpluses as:

$$E_x^B = x$$

$$E_y^B = y - 168$$

the Lagrangian is presented similarly to the one above, thus obtaining:

$$E_x^B = 84 \cdot \frac{p_y}{p_x} - 1$$

$$E_y^B = \frac{p_x}{p_y} - 84$$

and the corresponding budget straight line will be:

$$p_x \left(84 \frac{p_y}{p_x} - 1 \right) + p_y \left(\frac{p_x}{p_y} - 84 \right) = 0$$

Moreover, individuals A and B exchange goods x and y in perfect competition conditions until equilibrium is achieved. This equilibrium will be possible when:

$$E_x = E_x^A + E_x^B = \frac{p_y}{p_x} - 41,5 + 84 \frac{p_y}{p_x} - 1;$$

$$E_x = 85 \frac{p_y}{p_x} - 42,5 = 0 \qquad\qquad (3.1)$$

$$E_y = E_y^A + E_y^B = 41,5 \frac{p_x}{p_y} - 1 + \frac{p_x}{p_y} - 84;$$

$$E_y = 42,5 \frac{p_x}{p_y} - 85 = 0 \qquad\qquad (3.2)$$

From equation (3.1) we obtain:

$$\frac{p_y}{p_x} = 0,5$$

and from (3.2) it is possible to write:

$$\frac{p_x}{p_y} = 2$$

Therefore, solutions are identical since, in equilibrium, one unit of x can be replaced with two units of y. By substituting the price rates obtained, we have the equilibrium result in terms of the quantity exchanged. In other words:

$$E_x^A = -41$$

$$E_y^A = 82$$

$$E_x^B = 41$$

$$E_y^A = -82$$

Which means that consumer A gives 41 units of x to B and receives 82 units of y in exchange.

The geometry of this model is the Edgeworth's box.

3.5
The General Equilibrium Model with a Representative Agent with a Producer-Consumer (or of Robinson Crusoe)

Assume an economy formed by only one individual. This individual consumes a product x such that x is produced by a single factor of production L, labor. Assume also that, for exchanging or transferring these goods (x, L), there is a virtual auctioneer of the Walrasian type which fixes prices (P_x, w) by correcting any possible supply and demand surplus of every good.

As a producer, Robinson Crusoe will try to solve the following problem:

$$\left. \begin{array}{l} \max.\pi = p_x x_0 - wL \\ \text{with} \qquad x_0 = x(L) \end{array} \right\}$$

First order conditions require that the first partial derivatives with respect to L and λ equal zero, in other words:

$$\frac{\partial \pi}{\partial L} = \frac{\partial x(L)}{\partial L} p_x - w = 0$$

$$\frac{\partial \pi}{\partial \lambda} = x(L) - x_0 = 0$$

from where:

$$\frac{\partial x(L)}{\partial L} = \frac{w}{p_x}$$

$$MPg_L = \frac{w}{p_x} \text{ or } p_x MPg_L = w$$

Let's see now how Robinson Crusoe behaves when consuming:
The problem will be now:

$$\left. \begin{array}{l} \max.U(L, x) = U \\ \text{s.to} \quad R = p_x x + wL \end{array} \right\}$$

The auxiliary Lagrangian is now:

$$L = U(L, x) - \lambda(p_x x + wL - R)$$

and the first order conditions are:

$$
\left.
\begin{aligned}
\frac{\partial L}{\partial L} &= \frac{\partial U(L, x)}{\partial L} - \lambda w = 0 \\[2mm]
\frac{\partial L}{\partial x} &= \frac{\partial U(L, x)}{\partial x} - \lambda p_x = 0 \\[2mm]
\frac{\partial L}{\partial \lambda} &= -p_x x + wL - R = 0
\end{aligned}
\right\}
$$

$$\frac{\partial U(L, x)}{\partial L} = \lambda w; \quad \frac{\partial U(L, x)}{\partial x} = \lambda p_x$$

$$\frac{\partial U(L, x) \big/ \partial L}{\partial U(L, x) \big/ \partial x} = \frac{w}{p_x}$$

This rate is the same as the input-output rate of substitution of the general equilibrium model with production, with two agents-producers and for two goods, determined for one agent and one good.

3.6
The Equilibrium Production Model with Constant Returns to Scale

Assume a consumer with a Cobb-Douglas-type utility function, which depends on the consumption of goods x and H, the latter representing leisure time, such that it is possible to write:

$$U(x, H) = x^\alpha H^{1-\alpha}$$

The consumer is also a producer and has one unit of H, which enables him to dedicate it to the productive labor at wage w, with constant returns to scale technology of the type:

$$x = \alpha L$$

Therefore, the consumer will try to solve the problem:

$$
\left.
\begin{aligned}
&\max. U(x, H) = x^\alpha H^{1-\alpha} \\
&\text{s.to} \quad px = wH
\end{aligned}
\right\}
\max. \pi = p(\alpha L) - wH = 0
$$

where:

$$px = wH$$

since profits are null:

$$px = w - wH \Rightarrow px = w(1-H) \Rightarrow \frac{px}{1-H} = w$$

$$x(p, w) = \alpha \frac{w}{p} \; ; \; H(p, w) = (1 - \alpha) \, w/w = 1 - \alpha$$

The equilibrium labor supply is α and the level of production is α^2.

3.7
The Equilibrium Production Model with Decreasing Returns to Scale

Assume a Cobb-Douglas utility function like that in the above example:

$$U(x, H) = x^\alpha H^{1-\alpha}$$

and a production function:

$$x = \sqrt{L}$$

Assuming now that the price of x is p=1 (standardized), the profit maximization problem will be:

$$\max. \pi = \max.(L^{\frac{1}{2}} w - wL)$$

$$\frac{\partial (L^{\frac{1}{2}} - wL)}{\partial L} = \frac{1}{2} L^{-\frac{1}{2}} - w = 0$$

from which:

$$L^{-\frac{1}{2}} = 2w \Rightarrow L = (2w)^{-2} = \frac{1}{(2w)^2}$$

and from which:

$$x = \sqrt{L} = (L)^{\frac{1}{2}} = \left[\frac{1}{(2w)^2} \right]^{\frac{1}{2}} = \frac{1}{2w}$$

the profit function is found by replacing L with its value:

$$\pi(w) = (2w)^{-1} - w(2w)^{-2} = \frac{1}{4w}$$

Moreover, the consumer's income will include the income from the profits and therefore, leisure time demand H will be:

$$H(w) = \frac{(1-\alpha)}{w}\left(w + \frac{1}{4w}\right) = (1-\alpha)\left(1 + \frac{1}{4w^2}\right)$$

Now, it will be necessary to find a real wage which uses up the whole of the labor market:

$$\frac{1}{4w^2} = 1 - (1-\alpha)\left(1 + \frac{1}{4w^2}\right)$$

by finding the value of w in this equation:

$$w = \left(\frac{2-a}{4a}\right)^{\frac{1}{2}}$$

and substituting w in the profit function, we have:

$$\pi = \frac{1}{4}\left(\frac{2-a}{4a}\right)^{\frac{1}{2}}$$

Bibliographic References

Gravelle, H., Rees, R.: Microeconomics. 2nd ed. London: Logman Group, Ltd. 1995
Madden, P.: Concavity and Optimization in Microeconomics. Basil Blackwell, Ltd., Oxford, U.K. Journal of Economics 89, 488-500 (1986)
Varian, H..: Microeconomics Analysis. Norton & Norton 1991

4 Computable General Equilibrium

4.1
The Leontief Model

Assuming an economy with L consumers and N firms, n finished goods and x_i (i=1, ..., n) unfinished goods and m primary inputs y_k (k=1, ..., m), where technology presents constant returns to scale and has two types of constant or fixed coefficients (the Leontief technology).

Now, let a_{ij} be the quantity of product x_i necessary to produce one unit of x_j, and let b_{kj} be the quantity of primary resource y_k necessary to obtain one physical unit of product x_j, in other words:

$$x_j = \frac{x_{ij}}{a_{ij}} ; (i = 1,...,n)$$

$$x_j = \frac{y_{kj}}{b_{kj}} ; (k = 1,...,m; j = 1,...,n)$$

in terms of the Leontief production function we can write:

$$x_j = \min_{i,k} \left\{ \frac{x_{ij}}{a_{ij}} ; \frac{y_{kj}}{b_{kj}} \right\} ; (i, j = 1...n; R = 1...m)$$

The final demands for the goods

$$\vec{D} = (D_1,...D_n)$$

will require the production of the demands as well as of the unfinished goods necessary to produce those demands. In other words:

$$D_i + \sum_{j=1}^{n} x_{ij} = \hat{x}_i , (i = 1,...,n)$$

where:

$\hat{x}_i$ is the total production of finished and unfinished goods x_i ;

given that:

$$x_j = \frac{x_{ij}}{a_{ij}}$$

it is possible to ensure that:

$$x_j a_{ij} = x_{ij}$$

by taking addends:

$$\sum_{j=1}^{n} x_j a_{ij} = \sum_{j=1}^{n} x_{ij}$$

therefore, we can say:

$$D_i + \sum_{j=1}^{n} x_j a_{ij} = \hat{x}_i, (i = 1,...,n)$$

by denominating the matrix:

$$\sum_{j=1}^{n} a_{ij} = A$$

and the vector column of total production:

$$\sum_{j=1}^{n} x_j = \vec{x}$$

now we can say:

$$A\vec{x} + \vec{D} = \vec{x}$$

from where, by introducing identity matrix I:

$$(I - A)^{-1} \vec{D} = \vec{x}$$

Or, alternatively, by finding values at the above statement, it is possible to obtain final demand vector $\vec{D}$ such as:

$$\vec{D} = (I - A)\vec{x}$$

In the above statements, $(I-A)^{-1}$ is known as the Leontief inverse matrix, the a_{ij} of matrix A are known as the technical coefficients representing the direct multipliers. If we call r_{ij} the different items of the Leontief inverse matrix $(I-A)^{-1}$, these items represent the direct and indirect multipliers.

If the Leontief inverse matrix is extended by including a new column formed by private consumption and a new line formed by wages and salaries paid, the items of inverse matrix r_{ij} represent the direct, indirect and induced multipliers.

In addition to the final demands and the corresponding multipliers it is also possible to estimate the amounts of each primary input to produce each good. Since:

$$x_j = \frac{y_{kj}}{b_{kj}} (j = 1,..., n; k = 1,...m)$$

then:

$$x_j b_{kj} = y_{kj}$$

by taking addends:

$$\sum_{j=1}^{n} b_{kj} x_j = \sum y_{kj} = y_k \ (k = 1, ..., m)$$

If we denominate now:

$$\sum_{j=1}^{n} b_{kj} = B, \ \sum_{j=1}^{n} x_j = \vec{x},$$

and also $\vec{y}$ to vector y_k of primary inputs, then, it will be possible to write:

$$B\vec{x} = \vec{y}$$

Equation which provides the quantity of inputs necessary to produce goods x_j.

Moreover, the goods demand and resource supply functions of L consumers are:

$$\vec{D} = D(\vec{p}, \vec{w})$$

$$\vec{Y} = Y(\vec{p}, \vec{w})$$

where $\vec{w}$ represents the prices of resources and where it must be verified for all competitive equilibrium with constant returns to scale that:

$$\vec{p}A + \vec{w}B \geq \vec{p}$$

or that:

$$\vec{p}(I - A) \leq \vec{w}B$$

In short, an economy with L consumers, N firms and a Leontief technology given by matrices A and B with good demand functions of the type:

$$\vec{D} = D(\vec{p}, \vec{w})$$

and resource supply functions of the type:

$$\vec{Y} = Y(\vec{p}, \vec{w})$$

will have a competitive equilibrium if there exists a price vector $(\vec{p}*, \vec{w}*) \in S^{m+n}$ and an allocation $(x*, D*, y*)$ such that:

$$\vec{D}* = (I - A)\vec{x}*; x*, D*, y* > 0$$

$$B\vec{x}* \leq \vec{y}*;$$

$$p*(I - A) \leq \vec{w}*B;$$

$$D* = D(\vec{p}*, \vec{w}*);$$

$$y* = y(\vec{p}*, \vec{w}*);$$

The above system satisfies Hawkins-Simon conditions, which requires that all the main minors of $(I - A)$ are positive. Therefore, the existence of equilibrium in the Leontief model can be guaranteed.

Moreover, we must say that in the case of the Leontief model, competitive equilibrium and the demonstration of its existence can be alternatively exposed as a linear programming model. Thus, for certain prices of x_i given as $\vec{p}$ and certain known supplies of primary inputs $\vec{y}$, the maximization problem of the final demand or net output value subjected to resource restriction can be exposed as the primal:

$$\left.\begin{aligned} & \max \vec{p}(I - A)\vec{x} = \vec{p}D \\ & \text{s.to } B\vec{x} \le \vec{y} \\ & \quad \vec{x} > 0 \end{aligned}\right\}$$

or as the dual:

$$\left.\begin{aligned} & \min \vec{w}\,\vec{y} = \vec{C} \\ & \text{s.to } \vec{p}(I - A) \le \vec{w}B \\ & \quad \vec{w} > 0 \end{aligned}\right\}$$

which accounts for the minimization of the total production costs for the restrictions of a non-positive profit as well as for prices of the given goods and the quantity of given resources.

Both problems provide the same quantities of produced goods and consumed equilibrium inputs by the fundamental duality theorem and a price vector $\vec{p}$ also of equilibrium.

4.2
Applications. Economic Impact Models: Economic Impact Study*

4.2.1 Introduction

In two previous works -Villaverde Castro and Coto Millán (1995 and 1996)- some studies have been made of similar characteristics to the one here presented. This study will follow the methodology used in the last work as it is more suitable for the case of Santander and because at present it constitutes the most agreed methodology. Said methodology is considered the most agreed mainly due to the wide number of studies (we have reference of more than two hundred studies) which employ it, and secondly on its use by most Spanish ports, which, except for logical differences, will enable us to establish comparisons. Data in this work will refer to 1998 being the year about which the various associations have provided us with information through their surveys and the Register of Companies Reports.

---

* This work is a posterior version of the author on the book: Coto-Millán, P., Gallego, J. L. and Villaverde, J. (2001): Crecimiento Porturario y Desarrollo Regional. Aplicación al Puerto de Santander. Navalia Técnica. Ed. Autoridad Portuaria de Santander.

Port agents will be considered in two big groups: Port Industry and Industry Depending on the Port. Port Industry includes: the Port Authority, Customs and Other Port Industry; the third one of these includes at the same time: the State Stowage Society (SESTISAN), Stowing Societies, Shipping Agencies, Forwarding Agents, Towing Societies, Mooring Societies, Associations of Dock Pilots, Free deposits and others. In other words, port agents are all those economic agents who carry out the operations necessary to perform the loading and unloading movements of cargo and passengers, either being activities carried out at first line of port, at the docks or as second-line operations in the port precincts. The Industry Depending on the Port will include those firms of the regional economy related to port activity because they use the port services both when they require products, raw material and *inputs* to carry out their productive process and when they wish to sell their finished products through the port of Santander anywhere in the world. In addition to the demand rate of firms when they act as customers of the port, there is a supply rate when these firms supply goods and services to the port. Therefore, the addition of the effects of firms both as demanders and suppliers will give as a result the effects of the Industry Depending on the Port. The variables to be considered for the estimation of the economic impact of the port or Santander will be: number of jobs, sales, wages and salaries, gross exploitation surplus (GES), paid taxes and gross added value (GAV). This research will follow the procedure below in order to estimate the economic impact for 1998:

First, we will estimate the magnitude of each relevant variable for each one of the agents of Port Industry: jobs, sales, wages and salaries, GES, taxes and GAV.

Second, we will regionalize and update the latest national input-output table available.

Third, the indirect impact vector is calculated by sectors of activities through the classification into sectors of activities of the purchases and investments of the Port Authority and the rest of Port Industry.

Fourth, we estimate the indirect impacts of Port Industry from the indirect impact vector for 1994 in pesetas, by multiplying this vector by the product of the Technical Coefficient Matrix of the GAV for 1994, by the Inverse Regional Matrix for 1994 and the result obtained is multiplied by a deflator vector which enables us to convert it into pesetas for 1998. Once this vector in pesetas for 1998 is obtained, it is multiplied by the matrix of Indices related to the GAV of jobs, wages and salaries, GES, taxes and sales. Thus, we finally obtain the indirect effect impact in terms of the following magnitudes: jobs, sales, wages and salaries, GES, taxes and GAV.

Fifth, we calculate the induced impact vector from the classification into sectors of activities of wages and salaries of direct and indirect impacts.

Sixth, we estimate the induced impacts of Port Industry from the induced impact vector for 1994 in pesetas, by multiplying this vector by the product of the Technical Coefficient Matrix of the GAV for 1994, by the Regional Inverse Matrix for 1994 and the result obtained is multiplied by a deflator vector which enables us to convert pesetas for 1994 into pesetas for 1998. Once this vector in pesetas for 1998 is obtained, it is multiplied by the matrix of Indices related to the GAV of jobs, wages and salaries, GES, taxes and sales. Thus, we finally obtain the induced effects in terms of the following magnitudes: jobs, sales, wages and salaries, GES, taxes and GAV.

Seventh, the direct, indirect and induced effects of Port Industry are added and a summary of the total effects of Port Industry is presented.

Eighth, for the Industry Depending on the Port, we estimate the magnitude of each one of the relevant variables from a specific degree of port dependency (D.P.D) of the main customers.

Ninth, for the Industry Depending on the Port, we estimate the magnitude of the relevant variables from the classification of the main suppliers into sectors of activities.

Tenth, we aggregate the total of direct effects of both demanders and suppliers in the Industry Depending on the Port.

Eleventh, we estimate the indirect impact vector of the Industry Depending on the Port for suppliers from a Degree of Port Dependency (D.P.D.) of said suppliers.

Twelfth, we estimate the indirect impact vector for demanders from a specific Degree of Port Dependency (D.P.D.) of said demanders.

Thirteenth, we calculate the indirect impact of the Industry Depending on the Port from the indirect impact vector in pesetas for 1994, by multiplying this vector by the product of the Technical Coefficient Matrix of the GAV for 1994 by the Regional Inverse Matrix for 1994 and the result obtained is multiplied by a deflator vector which enables us to convert pesetas for 1994 into pesetas for 1998. Once the vector in pesetas for 1998 has been obtained, we multiply it by the matrix of Indices related to the GAV of jobs, wages and salaries, GES, taxes and sales. Thus we finally obtain the indirect effect impact in terms of the following magnitudes: jobs, sales, wages and salaries, GES, taxes and GAV.

Fourteenth, we estimate the induced impact vector of the Industry Depending on the Port by classifying the direct and indirect wages of this Industry into sectors of activities.

Fifteenth, we estimate the induced impacts of the Industry Depending on the Port from the induced impact vector, by multiplying this vector by the product of the Technical Coefficient Matrix of the GAV for 1994, by the Regional Inverse Matrix for 1994 and the result obtained is multiplied by a deflator vector which enables us to convert it into pesetas for 1998. Once the vector in pesetas for 1998 is obtained, we multiply it by the matrix of Indices related to the GAV of jobs, wages and salaries, GES, taxes and sales. Thus we finally obtain the induced effect impact in terms of the following magnitudes: jobs, sales, wages and salaries, GES, taxes and GAV.

Sixteenth, the direct, indirect and induced effects of the Industry Depending on the Port are added and a summary of the total effects of this Industry is presented.

Seventeenth, we add the direct, indirect and induced effects of Port Industry and the direct, indirect and induced effects of the Industry Depending on the Port, thus obtaining the total effects of the Port in Cantabrian economy.

Finally, these effects are discussed in relation with terms relative to Cantabrian economy.

4.2.2 Direct Effects of Port Industry

4.2.2.1 Port Authority

The direct effects of the Port Authority have been obtained from the Annual Report of 1998. Table 4.1 presents these effects for the magnitudes concerned in this impact study.

Table 4.1. Port Authority. Direct Effects 1998

Jobs	Sales	Wages	GES	Taxes	GAVfc
206	3187.96	921.5	1596.43	31.57	2517.93

4.2.2.2 Customs

Data in Table 4.2 have been provided by the Customs Authority in terms of employment and income, an estimation of the work developed by the different officials whose work is not exclusive to the port.

Table 4.2. Customs. Direct Effects 1998

Jobs	Sales	Wages	GES	Taxes	GAVfc
13	0	50	0	25000	50

4.2.2.3 Other Port Industry

In this chapter the following agents are considered:

SESTISAN
Stowing Society
Shipping Societies
Forwarding Agents
Dock Pilot Association
Towing Societies
Mooring Societies
Free Deposit
Others

The data summarized in Table 4.3 come mainly from surveys and from the accounting records of the Register of Companies. Further indirect information from the Chamber of Commerce and the Cantabrian delegation of the ICEX has also been used to complete these data.

Table 4.3. Other Port Industry. Direct Effects 1998

Activity	Jobs	Sales	Wages	GES	Taxes	GAVfc
Shipping agents	265	14227.43	1750.3	711.37	78	2461.67
Stevedors	233	7719.88	2324.77	1621.17	398	3945.94
Forwarding agents	13	312	215	78	12	293
Dock pilots	14	161	110	0	48	110
Free deposit	12	116	46	10	9.4	56
Sestisan	64	496	485	0	0	485
Towers	36	586	104	0	0	104
Mooring operators	16	67	52	0	0	52
Fishing and others	587	3162	1961	158.1	31.2	2119.1
Total	**1240**	**26847.31**	**7048.07**	**2578.64**	**576.6**	**9626.71**

4.2.2.4 Direct Effects of Port Industry

Table 4.4. Total of Port Industry. Direct Effects 1998

Activity	Jobs	Sales	Wages	GES	Taxes	GAVfc
Santander Port Authority	206	3187.96	921.5	1596.43	31.57	2517.93
Customs	13	0	50	0	25000	50
Other Port Industry	1240	26847.31	7048.07	2578.64	576.6	9626.71
Total	**1459**	**30035.27**	**8019.57**	**4175.07**	**25608.17**	**12194.64**

The addition of Tables 4.1, 4.2 and 4.3 gives Table 4.4, which represents the Direct Effects of Port Industry. It is worth mentioning here that these direct effects – in comparison with the study made for 1993 by Villaverde Castro and Coto Millán (1996) using the same methodology – have increased 5.75% for employment, about 48.05% for sales and 36.63% for wages and salaries. As regards the following variables we can see that the GES, taxes and the GAV have increased about 16% each.

Naturally, these growths have been calculated in constant pesetas, changing 1993 pesetas into 1998 pesetas. Growth figures in direct terms are quite eloquent themselves and they show that Port Industry has grown spectacularly in the last five years.

4.2.3 Indirect and Induced Effects of Port Industry

These effects have been estimated by using the information supplied by the national input-output table, once regionalized and updated for 1998. Results are presented in Tables 4.5, 4.6 and 4.7.

Table 4.5. National Matrix of Intermediate Inputs R16

R16	1	2	3	4	5	6	7	8	9	10	11	12	13	14	15	16	Total
1	630166	37	64	18440	122	145	2717716	48240	38582	111791	1576	226176	119	0	1016	41753	3835943
2	317696	1585137	376321	271036	114023	84088	145041	61886	67095	85951	162077	655872	507740	47171	66582	427862	4975578
3	3838	7730	928284	113742	777355	334022	81780	1709	14543	54332	1226227	55216	10036	0	1136	6480	3616430
4	252824	10111	121999	459967	105224	73385	76438	167306	128589	335085	111346	206383	5812	4938	14753	328776	2402936
5	143156	131771	163945	57431	1096347	668843	167806	38705	24052	82186	632550	245429	55422	26586	36420	453622	4024271
6	15652	21	0	0	9312	695935	0	0	0	263	794	393712	158935	0	4400	145791	1424815
7	819178	0	0	53137	0	0	615545	70598	2105	292	0	1567597	1148	932	90	130787	3261409
8	10903	1336	5291	14275	10515	46198	7515	464216	7546	45120	6400	66941	8414	1521	2307	68438	766936
9	1055	4137	34685	73469	36120	14022	164903	26162	417754	43295	22477	185976	28711	48595	167982	164688	1434031
10	27579	5749	20841	77231	138750	293975	156883	74583	17277	319905	235529	161009	123669	14283	12070	101668	1781001
11	8032	39427	19299	7303	14554	10251	15871	8270	4117	10058	0	359685	71781	61878	771075	181337	1582938
12	173091	101908	347511	94005	299891	73143	352204	119124	148307	145519	335749	857320	341007	71598	126303	334895	3921575
13	124562	64379	168896	120499	142765	143042	252846	66646	63140	100948	401892	554277	746107	215324	140964	395271	3701558
14	14101	33976	47542	58520	90853	77275	48610	45762	27399	71214	95336	148308	82492	4245570	92098	37332	5216388
15	142679	154245	125072	139601	258471	282956	189168	75060	74623	126650	608661	868659	199874	852692	397828	822116	5318355
16	5024	11248	11962	33193	45611	28740	15054	5327	5086	19240	8172	69987	39073	56597	43105	784401	1181820
Total	2689536	2151212	2371712	1591849	3139913	2826020	5007380	1273594	1040215	1551849	3848786	6622547	2380340	5647685	1878129	4425217	48445984
GAVimp	2162978	3713834	1437353	1030003	2462436	1174019	2663712	992070	744746	1078517	5159193	1460479	6377643	4047753	7424059	12427169	64900281
TR	5354904	7565797	4693567	4143956	9005199	6258003	9313200	3186122	2040448	3402270	9536795	22558452	6712169	5763521	11065669	16408381	127008453

Note: TR = Total resources

Table 4.6. National Matrix of Technical Coefficients, 1994

4 Computable General Equilibrium

	1	2	3	4	5	6	7	8	9	10	11	12	13	14	15	16
1	0.11768	0.00000	0.00001	0.00445	0.00001	0.00002	0.29181	0.01514	0.01891	0.03286	0.00017	0.01003	0.00002	0.00000	0.00009	0.00254
2	0.05933	0.20951	0.08018	0.06541	0.01266	0.01344	0.01557	0.01942	0.03288	0.02526	0.01699	0.02907	0.07564	0.00818	0.00602	0.02608
3	0.00072	0.00102	0.19778	0.02745	0.08632	0.05338	0.00878	0.00054	0.00713	0.01597	0.12858	0.00245	0.00150	0.00000	0.00010	0.00039
4	0.04721	0.00134	0.02599	0.11100	0.01168	0.01173	0.00821	0.05251	0.06302	0.09849	0.01168	0.00915	0.00087	0.00086	0.00133	0.02004
5	0.02673	0.01742	0.03493	0.01386	0.12175	0.10688	0.01802	0.01215	0.01179	0.02416	0.06633	0.01088	0.00826	0.00461	0.00329	0.02765
6	0.00292	0.00000	0.00000	0.00000	0.00103	0.11121	0.00000	0.00000	0.00000	0.00008	0.00008	0.01745	0.02368	0.00000	0.00040	0.00889
7	0.15298	0.00000	0.00000	0.01282	0.00000	0.00000	0.06609	0.02216	0.00103	0.00009	0.00000	0.06949	0.00017	0.00016	0.00001	0.00797
8	0.00204	0.00018	0.00113	0.00344	0.00117	0.00738	0.00081	0.14570	0.00370	0.01326	0.00067	0.00297	0.00125	0.00026	0.00021	0.00417
9	0.00020	0.00055	0.00739	0.01773	0.00401	0.00224	0.01771	0.00821	0.20474	0.01273	0.00236	0.00824	0.00428	0.00843	0.01518	0.01004
10	0.00515	0.00076	0.00444	0.01864	0.01541	0.04698	0.01685	0.02341	0.00847	0.09403	0.02470	0.00714	0.01842	0.00248	0.00109	0.00620
11	0.00150	0.00521	0.00411	0.00176	0.00162	0.00164	0.00170	0.00260	0.00202	0.00296	0.00000	0.01594	0.01069	0.01074	0.06968	0.01105
12	0.03232	0.01347	0.07404	0.02268	0.03330	0.01169	0.03782	0.03739	0.07268	0.04277	0.03521	0.03800	0.05080	0.01242	0.01141	0.02041
13	0.02326	0.00851	0.03598	0.02908	0.01585	0.02286	0.02715	0.02092	0.03094	0.02967	0.04214	0.02457	0.11116	0.03736	0.01274	0.02409
14	0.00263	0.00449	0.01013	0.01412	0.01009	0.01235	0.00522	0.01436	0.01343	0.02093	0.01000	0.00657	0.01229	0.73663	0.00832	0.00228
15	0.02664	0.02039	0.02665	0.03369	0.02870	0.04522	0.02031	0.02356	0.03657	0.03723	0.06382	0.03851	0.02978	0.14795	0.03595	0.05010
16	0.00094	0.00149	0.00255	0.00801	0.00506	0.00459	0.00162	0.00167	0.00249	0.00566	0.00086	0.00310	0.00582	0.00982	0.00390	0.04780
GAVmp	0.50226	0.28433	0.50531	0.38414	0.34868	0.45158	0.53766	0.39973	0.50980	0.45612	0.40357	0.29357	0.35463	0.97990	0.16973	0.26969

Table 4.7. Modified Location Coefficients

	Cantabria (C)	Spain (E)	%C	%E	Coefficients
1	31823	2136262	0.03797	0.03293	1.15311
2	14199	3716207	0.01694	0.05728	0.29576
3	38142	1442342	0.04551	0.02223	2.04701
4	19947	1045763	0.02380	0.01612	1.47648
5	50026	2506011	0.05969	0.03863	1.54524
6	11975	1163728	0.01429	0.01794	0.79654
7	44478	2680086	0.05307	0.04131	1.28464
8	3651	992797	0.00436	0.01530	0.28467
9	4314	746077	0.00515	0.01150	0.44759
10	12010	1080287	0.01433	0.01665	0.86057
11	62141	5150784	0.07414	0.07939	0.93387
12	148067	14607087	0.17666	0.22515	0.78465
13	41573	3717022	0.04960	0.05729	0.86577
14	45370	4047753	0.05413	0.06239	0.86764
15	190968	10867985	0.22785	0.16751	1.36018
16	119450	8977781	0.14252	0.13838	1.02991
Total	838134	64877972	1	1	

4.2.3.1 Regionalization of the National Input-Output Table

As is widely known, since there is not an Input-Output Table for Cantabria, the last Input-Output Table of Spanish Economy for 1994 has been adapted to Cantabria and then updated for 1998. In order to carry out regionalization, it is necessary to prepare the information of the Spanish Regional Accounts regarding Cantabria. The Spanish Regional Accounts classifies the information in seventeen sectors of activity while the Input-Output Table of Spanish Economy for 1994 presents this information for 57 sectors of activity. Moreover, in order to homogenize the data, sectors 17 (production imputed to bank services) and 14 (credit and insurance services) are aggregated in only one sector, 14 (credit and insurance services) in such a way that one table will be considered with the following 16 sectors of activities:

1. Agriculture, forestry and fishing
2. Energy
3. Minerals and metals and by-products
4. Chemical products
5. Metal products, machinery and electrical material
6. Transport material
7. Food, drinks and tobacco
8. Textile products, leather, shoes and clothes
9. Paper, goods made of paper and printing items

10. Diverse industries
11. Construction and civil engineering works
12. Recovering and repairing works. Commerce, catering industry and restaurants
13. Transport and communication services
14. Credit and insurance services
15. Other services concerning selling
16. General Administration services, teaching and research services, health service, house cleaning services and others not related to sales.

We have reduced the National Table to these 16 sectors of activities and added the line of GAV and Total Resources to make Table 4.5. Table 4.6 presents the matrix of technical coefficients in relation to this reduced table, obtained by dividing the value at each box of the transaction matrix by the Total Resources of each sector of activity. Once these estimations have been made, the national Table is regionalized. The method followed to do this is that of location coefficients. GAV location coefficients have been estimated at market prices for each one of the sectors of activities. These coefficients are presented in Table 4.7. With them we construct a matrix whose main diagonal is formed by said coefficients and the other items different from said main diagonal are zero. This matrix is multiplied by the national matrix of technical coefficients in table 4.6 to obtain the regional matrix of technical coefficients for Cantabria presented in Table 4.8. From the matrix in Table 4.8 we obtain the Leontief inverse regional matrix presented in Table 4.9.

Table 4.8. Regional Matrix of Technical Coefficients, 1994

	1	2	3	4	5	6	7	8	9	10	11	12	13	14	15	16
1	0.11768	0.00000	0.00001	0.00445	0.00001	0.00002	0.29181	0.01514	0.01891	0.03286	0.00017	0.01003	0.00002	0.00000	0.00009	0.00254
2	0.01755	0.06197	0.02371	0.01934	0.00374	0.00397	0.00461	0.00574	0.00973	0.00747	0.00503	0.00860	0.02237	0.00242	0.00178	0.00771
3	0.00072	0.00102	0.19778	0.02745	0.08632	0.05338	0.00878	0.00054	0.00713	0.01597	0.12858	0.00245	0.00150	0.00000	0.00010	0.00039
4	0.04721	0.00134	0.02599	0.11100	0.01168	0.01173	0.00821	0.05251	0.06302	0.09849	0.01168	0.00915	0.00087	0.00086	0.00133	0.02004
5	0.02673	0.01742	0.03493	0.01386	0.12175	0.10688	0.01802	0.01215	0.01179	0.02416	0.06633	0.01088	0.00826	0.00461	0.00329	0.02765
6	0.00233	0.00000	0.00000	0.00000	0.00082	0.08858	0.00000	0.00000	0.00000	0.00006	0.00007	0.01390	0.01886	0.00000	0.00032	0.00708
7	0.15298	0.00000	0.00000	0.01282	0.00000	0.00000	0.06609	0.02216	0.00103	0.00009	0.00000	0.06949	0.00017	0.00016	0.00001	0.00797
8	0.00058	0.00005	0.00032	0.00098	0.00033	0.00210	0.00023	0.04148	0.00105	0.00378	0.00019	0.00084	0.00036	0.00008	0.00006	0.00119
9	0.00009	0.00024	0.00331	0.00794	0.00180	0.00100	0.00793	0.00368	0.09164	0.00570	0.00105	0.00369	0.00191	0.00377	0.00679	0.00449
10	0.00443	0.00065	0.00382	0.01604	0.01326	0.04043	0.01450	0.02014	0.00729	0.08092	0.02125	0.00614	0.01586	0.00213	0.00094	0.00533
11	0.00140	0.00487	0.00384	0.00165	0.00151	0.00153	0.00159	0.00242	0.00188	0.00276	0.00000	0.01489	0.00999	0.01003	0.06507	0.01032
12	0.02536	0.01057	0.05810	0.01780	0.02613	0.00917	0.02967	0.02934	0.05703	0.03356	0.02762	0.02982	0.03986	0.00975	0.00896	0.01601
13	0.02014	0.00737	0.03115	0.02517	0.01373	0.01979	0.02350	0.01811	0.02679	0.02569	0.03648	0.02127	0.09624	0.03234	0.01103	0.02086
14	0.00228	0.00390	0.00879	0.01225	0.00875	0.01071	0.00453	0.01246	0.01165	0.01816	0.00867	0.00570	0.01066	0.63913	0.00722	0.00197
15	0.02664	0.02039	0.02665	0.03369	0.02870	0.04522	0.02031	0.02356	0.03657	0.03723	0.06382	0.03851	0.02978	0.14795	0.03595	0.05010
16	0.00094	0.00149	0.00255	0.00801	0.00506	0.00459	0.00162	0.00167	0.00249	0.00566	0.00086	0.00310	0.00582	0.00982	0.00390	0.04780
GAVmp	0.502257	0.284334	0.505311	0.384138	0.348678	0.451585	0.537665	0.399732	0.509797	0.456122	0.403572	0.293573	0.354631	0.979902	0.169726	0.269692

Table 4.9. Regional Inverse Matrix, 1994

	1	2	3	4	5	6	7	8	9	10	11	12	13	14	15	16
1	1.20130	0.00067	0.00412	0.01385	0.00276	0.00356	0.37798	0.03099	0.02962	0.04665	0.00343	0.04036	0.00307	0.00297	0.00110	0.00807
2	0.02707	1.06691	0.03535	0.02675	0.00981	0.01008	0.01615	0.01042	0.01640	0.01528	0.01295	0.01273	0.02815	0.01264	0.00363	0.01115
3	0.01248	0.00525	1.25645	0.04354	0.12611	0.09188	0.02046	0.00761	0.01720	0.03249	0.17277	0.01170	0.00900	0.01357	0.01283	0.00927
4	0.06915	0.00272	0.04057	1.13157	0.02221	0.02624	0.03598	0.06818	0.08336	0.12721	0.02379	0.01670	0.00584	0.00882	0.00438	0.02728
5	0.04559	0.02266	0.05509	0.02398	1.14711	0.14170	0.03970	0.02042	0.02147	0.03844	0.08661	0.02154	0.01766	0.02540	0.01083	0.03818
6	0.00463	0.00049	0.00243	0.00142	0.00232	1.09854	0.00277	0.00135	0.00214	0.00197	0.00204	0.01670	0.02390	0.00339	0.00102	0.00921
7	0.20109	0.00120	0.00744	0.02017	0.00400	0.00300	1.13713	0.03375	0.01273	0.01336	0.00444	0.08429	0.00460	0.00456	0.00140	0.01246
8	0.00099	0.00010	0.00064	0.00136	0.00061	0.00278	0.00074	1.04355	0.00148	0.00459	0.00051	0.00110	0.00064	0.00047	0.00015	0.00146
9	0.00343	0.00076	0.00620	0.01128	0.00387	0.00338	0.01137	0.00609	1.10297	0.00942	0.00352	0.00590	0.00345	0.01582	0.00829	0.00643
10	0.01238	0.00173	0.00891	0.02212	0.01877	0.05257	0.02270	0.02628	0.01266	1.09323	0.02735	0.01109	0.02167	0.01163	0.00359	0.00903
11	0.00689	0.00751	0.01072	0.00729	0.00687	0.00846	0.00728	0.00700	0.00839	0.00980	1.00824	0.02001	0.01574	0.05901	0.06905	0.01603
12	0.04427	0.01385	0.08225	0.02972	0.04230	0.02553	0.05208	0.03934	0.07287	0.04911	0.04680	1.03971	0.04998	0.04227	0.01460	0.02336
13	0.03849	0.01093	0.05086	0.03899	0.02666	0.03562	0.04456	0.02937	0.04199	0.04317	0.05343	0.03214	1.11284	0.11156	0.01812	0.02960
14	0.01809	0.01372	0.03867	0.04521	0.03562	0.04534	0.02442	0.04384	0.04447	0.06586	0.03719	0.02308	0.03821	2.78812	0.02471	0.01204
15	0.04934	0.02725	0.05129	0.05460	0.04861	0.07185	0.04710	0.04166	0.05978	0.06569	0.08610	0.05380	0.04755	0.44167	1.04853	0.06353
16	0.00331	0.00221	0.00535	0.01105	0.00766	0.00794	0.00397	0.00375	0.00512	0.00937	0.00346	0.00471	0.00804	0.03184	0.00495	1.05148

4.2.3.2 Indirect and Induced Impact Vectors

The indirect effects of Port Industry are obtained by estimating the generation of employment and added value of main suppliers in Port Industry. In order to obtain said information it is necessary to know the purchases and investments of Port Industry in relation with other sectors of activities in the economy. For the case of Santander Port Authority, this information is known for each firm and it is relatively easy to classify each firm into its corresponding sector of activity. However, for the rest of Port Industry this task is not possible with the information available from surveys and accounts records. Therefore, we have proceeded to the sectorial disaggregation of the purchases of the sectors concerned with maritime transport, as depicted in Table 4.10. Something similar to the case of purchases happens with investment disaggregation and the same procedure is followed to obtain Table 4.11. Moreover, in order to know the induced effects, it is necessary to obtain the expenses in private consumption of the agents concerned in direct and indirect effects. Such expenses are found through the internal sectorial disaggregatation of private consumption in Table 4.12.

Table 4.10. Sectorial Dissagregation of the Purchases of Sectors Related to Maritime Transport

	Internal	Total	% Internal	Int/Total	Coefficient
1	119	119	0.042	1.000	0.0004
2	24631	43431	8.659	0.567	0.0491
3	6001	6400	2.110	0.938	0.0198
4	1303	1992	0.458	0.654	0.0030
5	16570	21436	5.825	0.773	0.0450
6	14313	14569	5.032	0.982	0.0494
7	685	768	0.241	0.892	0.0021
8	1993	2621	0.701	0.760	0.0053
9	9246	10332	3.250	0.895	0.0291
10	6171	6592	2.169	0.936	0.0203
11	27507	27507	9.670	1.000	0.0967
12	22285	22285	7.834	1.000	0.0783
13	77851	108962	27.368	0.714	0.1955
14	16907	16907	5.944	1.000	0.0594
15	55447	69668	19.492	0.796	0.1551
16	3428	3428	1.205	1.000	0.0121
Total	284457	357017	100.000	0.797	0.7968

Table 4.11. Sectorial Dissagregation of Investments

	Internal (I)	Total (T)	% Internal	I/T	Coefficient
1	3517	11969	0.093	0.294	0.0003
2	0	0	0.000	0.000	0.0000
3	22244	22244	0.173	1.000	0.0017
4	0	0	0.000	0.000	0.0000
5	1018673	2336818	18.172	0.436	0.0792
6	489005	1070593	8.325	0.457	0.0380
7	0	0	0.000	0.000	0.0000
8	11733	12749	0.099	0.920	0.0009
9	0	0	0.000	0.000	0.0000
10	276399	307124	2.388	0.900	0.0215
11	7828119	7828119	60.874	1.000	0.6087
12	240701	240701	1.872	1.000	0.0187
13	51443	51443	0.400	1.000	0.0040
14	0	0	0.000	0.000	0.0000
15	964961	964961	7.504	1.000	0.0750
16	12189	12918	0.100	0.944	0.0009
Total	10918984	12859639	100.000	0.849	0.8491

Table 4.12. Internal Sectorial Dissagregation of Private Consumption

	Internal Consumption				
	Internal(I)	Total Consumption (I)	(T/I)%	I/T	Percentages
1	566548	785617	1.442	0.721	0.0104
2	2260561	2265649	5.754	0.998	0.0574
3	9288	49252	0.024	0.189	0.0000
4	719357	960106	1.831	0.749	0.0137
5	368592	824485	0.938	0.447	0.0042
6	432199	1334661	1.100	0.324	0.0036
7	4293448	5229393	10.929	0.821	0.0897
8	1235515	1741248	3.145	0.710	0.0223
9	275541	340977	0.701	0.808	0.0057
10	532451	783864	1.355	0.679	0.0092
11	125738	125738	0.320	1.000	0.0032
12	17796874	17796874	45.303	1.000	0.4530
13	1907440	1959321	4.855	0.974	0.0473
14	429966	433880	1.094	0.991	0.0108
15	4192825	4212451	10.673	0.995	0.1062
16	4138161	4202336	10.534	0.985	0.1037
Total	39284504	43045852	100.000	0.913	0.9126

The Purchases and Investments which have been disaggregated into sectors for Santander Port Authority in 1998 are presented in Table 4.13. Table 4.14 shows the Purchases and Investments of the rest of Port Industry and in Table 4.15 the sectorial disaggregation related to the Rest of Port Industry is demonstrated. Finally, the indirect and induced impact vectors are presented in Tables 4.16 and 4.17.

Table 4.13. Purchases and Investments. Santander Port Authority

	Purchases	Investments	Total
1	0	0	0
2	97.668	38.214	135.882
3	0	8.123	8.123
4	0	0	0
5	3.453	16.373	19.826
6	20.854	1.309	22.163
7	0.078	0	0.078
8	0	0.053	0.053
9	10.005	1.166	11.171
10	6.011	7.311	13.322
11	169.21	848.35	1017.56
12	72.962	0	72.962
13	43.171	82.814	125.985
14	7.377	1.183	8.56
15	84.899	0.15	85.049
16	68.996	16.787	85.783
Total	584.684	1021.833	1606.517

Table 4.14. Purchases and Investments. Rest of Port Industry

Purchases	Investments
7196.3	2351.2

Table 4.15. Purchases and Investments. Rest of Port Industry by Sectors

	Purchases	Investments	Purchases	Investments	Total	Tot. Defl. Pts. 94
1	0.00042	0.00027	3.01	0.64	3.65	3.25
2	0.04911	0.00000	353.39	0.00	353.39	454.77
3	0.01978	0.00173	142.35	4.07	146.42	137.94
4	0.00300	0.00000	21.56	0.00	21.56	19.25
5	0.04503	0.07921	324.04	186.25	510.29	473.18
6	0.04943	0.03803	355.73	89.41	445.14	417.12
7	0.00215	0.00000	15.46	0.00	15.46	13.87
8	0.00533	0.00091	38.34	2.15	40.48	36.18
9	0.02909	0.00000	209.32	0.00	209.32	196.81
10	0.02031	0.02149	146.15	50.54	196.68	187.45
11	0.09670	0.60874	695.88	1431.26	2127.14	2815.15
12	0.07834	0.01872	563.77	44.01	607.78	578.89
13	0.19554	0.00400	1407.17	9.41	1416.57	1311.76
14	0.05944	0.00000	427.72	0.00	427.72	371.00
15	0.15513	0.07504	1116.39	176.43	1292.82	1171.71
16	0.01205	0.00095	86.72	2.23	88.95	153.32
			5907.005	1996.37915	7903.384033	

Table 4.16. Indirect Impact Vector of Port Industry

	APSAN	RIPORT	TOTAL	TDP 98
1	0	3.65	3.65	3.24
2	135.882	353.39	489.27	454.76
3	8.123	146.42	154.54	137.94
4	0	21.56	21.56	19.24
5	19.826	510.29	530.11	473.17
6	22.163	445.14	467.30	417.11
7	0.078	15.46	15.53	13.86
8	0.053	40.48	40.54	36.18
9	11.171	209.32	220.49	196.81
10	13.322	196.68	210.00	187.44
11	1017.56	2127.14	3144.70	2815.14
12	72.962	607.78	680.75	578.89
13	125.985	1416.57	1542.56	1311.00
14	8.56	427.72	436.28	371.00
15	85.049	1292.82	1377.87	1171.70
16	85.783	88.95	174.73	153.2
Total			9509.901	

Table 4.17. Induced Impact Vector of Port Industry

	Private Consumption	Total P 98
1	0.0104	36.36
2	0.057	209.93
3	0	0.16
4	0.0137	48.18
5	0.0041	14.73
6	0.0035	12.51
7	0.0897	315.08
8	0.022	78.36
9	0.005	19.90
10	0.009	32.33
11	0.003	11.27
12	0.453	1515.52
13	0.047	158.13
14	0.01	36.28
15	0.106	355.38
16	0.103	358.06

4.2.3.3 Indirect and Induced Effects of Port Industry

Whenever indirect and induced impact vectors are available it is possible to estimate the indirect and induced effects. In order to do this the following procedure will be followed:

First; a matrix is made in which the elements of the main diagonal are the added value coefficients obtained from the national matrix of technical coefficients. The remaining boxes are zero.

Second; the matrix previously obtained is multiplied by the Leontief regional inverse matrix and by the indirect impact vector (induced if applicable), thus obtaining an added value vector in pesetas for 1994, to which the corresponding deflator is applied to obtain pesetas for 1998.

Third; the ratios of wages and salaries, employment, taxes and EBE are estimated for each sector of activity with the information provided by the Spanish Regional Accounts for Cantabria.

Fourth; by multiplying the added value vector at input cost, deflated in pesetas for 1998, by each one of the ratio vectors previously obtained, we obtain the indirect impact values (induced if applicable) for the various economic magnitudes considered in this study.

Indirect and induced effects are presented in Tables 4.18 and 4.19.

Table 4.18. Indirect Effects. Port Industry

	Wages	Employment	Taxes	Sales	GES	GAV
1	5.6858954	0.02207755	0.05180208	96.0007	38.1963742	39.2499456
2	72.707479	0.01287542	0.95278085	372.811697	89.538573	182.818044
3	281.428971	0.07342986	1.79361464	1489.33126	183.326788	459.141272
4	46.5100238	0.01067968	0.37378894	327.611002	33.0866465	81.9337141
5	261.483483	0.08078638	1.35133583	987.000644	107.210549	367.401772
6	238.294882	0.06049739	5.96331377	1147.71337	34.9517131	258.734356
7	33.6211701	0.01086877	13.5710134	211.116383	29.1322809	60.4276237
8	18.8932584	0.00593788	0.07017496	62.7049586	5.76099302	19.7083676
9	106.285249	0.02735785	1.12851134	402.312772	50.04027	147.527209
10	126.967376	0.04952409	1.2071496	531.960935	59.0188971	185.870086
11	850.762318	0.3255385	58.1194736	446.649942	524.855167	1348.6192
12	88.6350319	0.07831412	3.0837512	480.205276	218.92202	314.247618
13	356.729991	0.14958339	15.292702	1289.96067	432.283777	731.603567
14	638.202083	0.10934927	3.74438398	2140.6447	799.244031	1503.38673
15	56.2912271	0.02785363	23.5123061	499.09683	289.766277	366.838078
16	59.0440644	0.01820107	0	86.6576004	13.5177388	65.6833323
Total	3241.5425	1.06287485	130.216102	10571.7787	2908.8521	6133.19092

Table 4.19. Induced Effects. Port Industry

Sectors	Employment	Sales	Wages	GES	Taxes	GAV
1	74.158	322.466	19.099	128.301	0.174	131.840
2	5.664	163.994	31.983	39.387	0.419	80.419
3	4.053	82.201	15.533	10.118	0.099	25.342
4	6.667	204.531	29.037	20.656	0.233	51.152
5	8.321	101.659	26.932	11.042	0.139	37.842
6	5.690	107.950	22.413	3.287	0.561	24.336
7	54.593	1060.429	168.878	146.330	68.167	303.525
8	11.431	120.713	36.371	11.091	0.135	37.941
9	4.512	66.347	17.528	8.252	0.186	24.329
10	9.952	106.904	25.516	11.861	0.243	37.353
11	8.957	12.290	23.409	14.442	1.599	37.108
12	140.120	859.187	158.586	391.697	5.517	562.254
13	23.138	199.531	55.179	66.866	2.365	113.165
14	14.805	289.831	86.409	108.213	0.507	203.550
15	8.102	145.175	16.374	84.286	6.839	106.704
16	33.313	158.609	108.068	24.741	0.000	120.220
Total	413.478	4001.816	841.315	1080.571	87.184	1897.079

4.2.3.4 Total Effects of Port Industry

Table 4.20 presents the total effects of Port Industry. We must say here that employment, both in absolute and relative terms, has decreased with respect to the research done by Villaverde Castro and Coto Millán (1996) for 1993. In absolute terms, employment has decreased by 665 jobs, in other words, they have fallen by 18.5% as compared with 1993. In 1993 Port Industry represented 2% of regional employment while in 1998 it represented 1.7% of regional employment. Also the GES showed a slight decrease of 2.7% with respect to 1993. However, this has not happened in the case of the remaining variables. The GAV has increased 10% as compared with 1998, signifying that it keeps its share of about 2% of the regional GAV. Something similar, even more positive, has occurred regarding the remaining variables: sales, wages and salaries and taxes. The reasons for this remarkable decrease in employment are specific. Undoubtedly, the fall in employment mainly affects the fishing sector. Employment in this field has fallen during the last five years in about three hundred jobs, in other words, around 60% of jobs have been lost. On the other hand, customs officials have decreased by half (from 29 to 13 officials employed) as a consequence of liberalization and the same has happened in the case of official workers who have passed from 31 to 13. In the Port Authority itself employment has also been reduced; from 234 to 206 workers. This direct fall in the activity together with other indirect and induced effects can explain the reduction of employment in the Port Industry.

Table 4.20. Total Effects. Port Industry

	Jobs	Sales	Wages	GES	Taxes	GAVfc
Total Direct	1459.0	30035.3	8019.6	4175.1	25608.2	12194.6
Total Indirect	1062.9	10571.8	3241.5	2908.9	263.0	6133.2
Total Induced	413.5	4001.8	841.3	1080.6	176.1	1897.1
Total 1998	2935.3	44608.9	12102.4	8164.5	26047.3	20224.9
Total 1993	3601.0	33349.0	8557.8	7230.9	11208.2	15831.1
Total 1993 (pesetas 1998)	3601.0	38718.2	9935.6	8395.1	13012.7	18379.9
Variation (%)	-18.5	15.2	21.8	-2.7	100.2	10.0

4.2.4 Direct Effects of the Industry Depending on the Port

As pointed out at the beginning of this chapter, there are two aspects in the Industry Depending on the Port: one related with demand and another one concerning supply. Undoubtedly, the demand aspect refers to customers' service and assistance. Moreover, supply is related to the companies which provide the port of Santander with their services. The customers are the main companies of Cantabrian region. In order to estimate first the customers' effective demand we will take into account that, as mentioned in chapter 2 of this work, national coastal traffic for 1998 represented only 5.3% of maritime traffic while the rest corresponded to external navigation. In other words, sea imports and exports represent 94.7%. Besides, a sample of the most significant 63 companies has been taken to represent the customer of the port of Santander, which has already been used for 1993. The sample accounts for 84.2% of the imports and 76.3% of the exports and it has been completed with data from the Register of Companies of Santander and of other Spanish cities whenever necessary. Moreover, surveys to the main companies have been made to complete the information. Table 4.21 has been elaborated with all these data. However, in order to have an idea of the degree of port dependency (DPD) of companies we have used the DPD for 1993 since we consider that responses do not vary too much in such a short period of time. All this information has been used to elaborate Table 4.22. As regards the supply aspect, shipyards are highly important among supply companies. Although they do not offer a port service in itself it is certain that their activity is very much connected with the existence of ports. Data appearing in Table 4.23 for these companies have been again obtained from the Register of Companies surveys. We have had to classify these data into sectors according to the afore-mentioned Purchase and Investment coefficients.

Table 4.21. Industry Depending on the Port. Direct Effects. Demanders (Original Data 1998)

Sectors	Jobs	Wages	GES	Sales	GAVfc
1	562	1305467	6882214	12529352	8187682
2	612	8104777	4649177	20248000	12753954
3	1814	7481444	4525870	86634000	12007314
4	3001	27029248	47585134	161221248	74614382
5	3997	17977668	11856305	140502377	29833973
6	3266	15455200	9603158	53282000	25058358
7	2713	10743000	12282138	40934000	23025138
8	550	8751432	4706313	15858186	13457745
9	0	0	0	0	0
10	638	20202000	-32510000	13768000	-12308000
11	589	2731475	3694988	9112308	6426463
12	0	0	0	0	0
13	629	1504000	-912216	2748000	591784
14	0	0	0	0	0
15	7	187657	51847	2653421	239504
16	0	0	0	0	0
Total	18378	121473368	72414928.1	559490893	193888297

Table 4.22. Industry Depending on the Port. Direct Effects. Demanders (Transformed Data 1998)

Sectors	DPD	Jobs	Sales	Wages	GES	Taxes	GAVfc
1	0.1	56.2	1252.9	130.5	688.2	13.4	818.8
2	0.5	306.0	10124.0	4052.4	2324.6	0.0	6377.0
3	1	1814.0	86634.0	7481.4	4525.9	6.8	12007.3
4	0.8	2400.8	128977.0	21623.4	38068.1	2749.3	59691.5
5	1	3997.0	140502.4	17977.7	11856.3	608.5	29834.0
6	0.3	979.8	15984.6	4636.6	2880.9	7.2	7517.5
7	0.1	271.3	4093.4	1074.3	1228.2	4.8	2302.5
8	0.1	55.0	1585.8	875.1	470.6	22.2	1345.8
9	0.1	0.0	0.0	0.0	0.0	0.0	0.0
10	0.1	63.8	1376.8	2020.2	-3251.0	0.0	-1230.8
11	0.1	58.9	911.2	273.1	369.5	61.6	642.6
12	0.1	0.0	0.0	0.0	0.0	0.0	0.0
13	0.3	188.7	824.4	451.2	-273.7	6.8	177.5
14	0	0.0	0.0	0.0	0.0	0.0	0.0
15	0	0.0	0.0	0.0	0.0	0.0	0.0
16	0	0.0	0.0	0.0	0.0	0.0	0.0
Total		10191.5	392266.6	60596.0	58887.7	3480.6	119483.7

Table 4.23. Industry Depending on the Port. Direct Effects. Suppliers (Transformed Data 1998)

Sectors	Jobs	Sales	Wages	GES	Taxes	GAVfc
Shipyards (A)	358	5704.33	1881.17	177.38	0	2058.45
Total without A	111	1248	471.4	93.6	28.3	565
Total	469	6952.33	2352.57	270.98	28.3	2623.45
1	0.00	0.00	0.00	0.00	0.00	0.00
2	22.20	249.60	94.28	18.72	5.66	113.00
3	7.77	87.36	33.00	6.55	1.98	39.55
4	5.55	62.40	23.57	4.68	1.42	28.25
5	18.87	212.16	80.14	15.91	4.81	96.05
6	8.88	99.84	37.71	7.49	2.26	45.20
7	2.22	24.96	9.43	1.87	0.57	11.30
8	4.44	49.92	18.86	3.74	1.13	22.60
9	52.17	586.56	221.56	43.99	13.30	265.55
10	15.54	174.72	66.00	13.10	3.96	79.10
11	52.17	586.56	221.56	43.99	13.30	265.55
12	11.10	124.80	47.14	9.36	2.83	56.50
13	54.39	611.52	230.99	45.86	13.87	276.85
14	14.43	162.24	61.28	12.17	3.68	73.45
15	64.38	723.84	273.41	54.29	16.41	327.70
16	5.55	62.40	23.57	4.68	1.42	28.25
Total without A	339.66	3818.88	1442.48	286.42	86.60	1728.90
Shipyard	358.00	5704.33	1881.17	177.38	0.00	2058.45
Total	697.66	9523.21	3323.65	463.80	86.60	3787.35

The addition of the results obtained for customers and suppliers is presented in Table 4.24.

Table 4.24. Industry Depending on the Port. Direct Effects. Customers and Suppliers

	Wages	Sales	Wages	GES	Taxes	GAVfc
Customers	10191.50	392266.56	60596.00	58887.72	3480.60	119483.71
Suppliers	697.66	9523.21	3323.65	463.80	86.60	3787.35
Total	10889.16	401789.77	63919.65	59351.51	3567.20	123271.06

4.2.5 Indirect and Induced Effects of the Industry Depending on the Port

The development of indirect and induced impact vectors for the Industry Depending on the Port is very similar to the elaboration of said vectors already carried out for the Port Industry. The only specific point here is that we must estimate the effects for both customers and suppliers.

4.2.5.1 Indirect and Induced Impact Vectors

For the case of suppliers, shipyards are separately assigned a unit degree of port dependency (DPD) for obvious reasons, while two choices are applied to the remaining sectors: choice 1, where the DPD of year 1993 is considered; choice 2, where DPD = 0, and companies with the latter degree are not considered. Choice 1 has been used to elaborate Table 4.25 and choice 2 equals this Table but for column DPD, which would have zero in all boxes as well as the total column, which would also have zero in all boxes except for the case of shipyards.

As far as customers are concerned, we have proceeded to classify Purchases and Investments into sectors in accordance with the estimated coefficients, and then we have applied the same degree of dependency previously applied, thus obtaining Table 4.26. If we continue with choice 2, we obtain Tables 4.27 and 4.28 with indirect and induced impact vectors. Table 4.29 shows the difference between choice 1 and choice 2 impact vectors.

Table 4.25. Indirect Impact Vector. Industry Depending on the Port. Suppliers

	Shipyards not included					Shipyards			
Sectors	Purchases	Investments	Total	DPD	Total	Purchases	Investments	Total	Total
	634.7	0				3823.73	525.4		
1	0.317	0.000	0.317	0.003	0.001	1.912	0.158	2.069	2.070
2	59.281	0.000	59.281	6.725	398.671	357.136	0.000	357.136	755.807
3	13.138	0.000	13.138	0.201	2.636	79.151	0.998	80.149	82.785
4	3.618	0.000	3.618	0.159	0.574	21.795	0.000	21.795	22.369
5	32.941	0.000	32.941	0.960	31.617	198.452	53.381	251.832	283.449
6	34.274	0.000	34.274	4.017	137.692	206.481	29.790	236.272	373.963
7	1.587	0.000	1.587	0.015	0.024	9.559	0.000	9.559	9.583
8	4.252	0.000	4.252	0.261	1.109	25.619	0.841	26.460	27.569
9	16.058	0.000	16.058	1.482	23.801	96.740	0.000	96.740	120.541
10	10.853	0.000	10.853	3.425	37.176	65.386	12.347	77.733	114.909
11	44.746	0.000	44.746	4.352	194.727	269.573	283.663	553.236	747.964
12	35.797	0.000	35.797	1.395	49.926	215.658	10.718	226.377	276.303
13	140.903	0.000	140.903	10.823	1524.955	848.868	2.680	851.548	2376.503
14	20.247	0.000	20.247	0.949	19.206	121.977	0.000	121.977	141.183
15	84.034	0.000	84.034	2.213	185.955	506.262	35.465	541.726	727.682
16	5.141	0.000	5.141	0.215	1.107	30.972	0.210	31.182	32.290

Table 4.26. Indirect Impact Vector. Industry Depending on the Port. Suppliers

Sectors	Purchases	Investments	Total	DPD	Total
	302391.61	14099.34			
1	151.20	4.23	155.43	0.1	15.54
2	28243.38	0.00	28243.38	0.5	14121.69
3	6259.51	26.79	6286.30	1	6286.30
4	1723.63	0.00	1723.63	0.8	1378.91
5	15694.12	1432.49	17126.62	1	17126.62
6	16329.15	799.43	17128.58	0.3	5138.57
7	755.98	0.00	755.98	0.1	75.60
8	2026.02	22.56	2048.58	0.1	204.86
9	7650.51	0.00	7650.51	0.1	765.05
10	5170.90	331.33	5502.23	0.1	550.22
11	21318.61	7612.23	28930.84	0.1	2893.08
12	17054.89	287.63	17342.51	0.1	1734.25
13	67130.94	71.91	67202.84	0.3	20160.85
14	9646.29	0.00	9646.29	0	0.00
15	40036.65	951.71	40988.35	0	0.00
16	2449.37	5.64	2455.01	0	0.00

Table 4.27. Indirect Impact Vector. Industry Depending on the Port. Total

Sectors	Customers	Suppliers	Total
1	15.54	2.07	17.61
2	14121.69	755.81	14877.50
3	6286.30	82.79	6369.08
4	1378.91	22.37	1401.28
5	17126.62	283.45	17410.07
6	5138.57	373.96	5512.54
7	75.60	9.58	85.18
8	204.86	27.57	232.43
9	765.05	120.54	885.59
10	550.22	114.91	665.13
11	2893.08	747.96	3641.05
12	1734.25	276.30	2010.55
13	20160.85	2376.50	22537.36
14	0.00	141.18	141.18
15	0.00	727.68	727.68
16	0.00	32.29	32.29

Table 4.28. Induced Impact Vector. Industry Depending on the Port

Sectors	Direct	Indirect	Total
1	664.78	277.70	942.48
2	3669.89	1533.04	5202.93
3	2.85	1.19	4.04
4	876.97	366.34	1243.31
5	268.12	112.00	380.12
6	227.72	95.13	322.85
7	5735.54	2395.93	8131.47
8	1426.42	595.87	2022.29
9	362.29	151.34	513.64
10	588.48	245.83	834.31
11	204.59	85.46	290.05
12	28957.22	12096.43	41053.65
13	3021.41	1262.15	4283.55
14	693.28	289.61	982.89
15	6790.34	2836.56	9626.90
16	6630.36	2769.73	9400.09
Direct wages 63919.7			
Indirect wages: 26701.4			

Table 4.29. Indirect Impact Vector. Industry Depending on the Port (1998)

Sectors	Choice 1	Choice 2
1	17.61	17.61
2	14478.82	14877.50
3	6366.44	6369.08
4	1400.70	1401.28
5	17378.45	17410.07
6	5374.85	5512.54
7	85.16	85.18
8	231.32	232.43
9	861.79	885.59
10	627.96	665.13
11	3446.32	3641.05
12	1960.63	2010.55
13	21012.40	22537.36
14	121.98	141.18
15	541.73	727.68
16	31.18	32.29

4.2.5.2 Indirect and Induced Effects of the Industry Depending on the Port

In table 4.30 we can observe the differences between induced impact vectors in choice 1 and choice 2. Table 4.31 shows the indirect effects of the Industry Depending on the Port in choice 1 while Table 4.32 presents the same indirect effects in choice 2. Table 4.33 shows the induced effects of the Industry Depending on the Port in choice 1 and Table 4.34 presents the induced effects corresponding to choice 2.

Table 4.30. Induced Impact Vector. Industry Depending on the Port (1998)

Sectors	Choice 1	Choice 2
1	934.34	942.48
2	5158.01	5202.93
3	4.01	4.04
4	1232.57	1243.31
5	376.84	380.12
6	320.07	322.85
7	8061.27	8131.47
8	2004.83	2022.29
9	509.20	513.64
10	827.11	834.31
11	287.55	290.05
12	40699.23	41053.65
13	4246.57	4283.55
14	974.41	982.89
15	9543.80	9626.90
16	9318.94	9400.09

Table 4.31. Indirect Effects of the Industry Depending on the Port (1998)-Choice 1

Sectors	Employment	Sales	Wages	GES	Taxes	GAV
1	125.34	545.04	32.28	216.86	0.29	222.84
2	358.23	10372.76	2022.94	2491.24	26.51	5086.56
3	1057.19	21442.23	4051.79	2639.40	25.82	6610.36
4	158.36	4857.91	689.66	490.62	5.54	1214.94
5	1905.35	23278.44	6167.10	2528.56	31.87	8665.18
6	770.83	14623.70	3036.26	445.34	75.98	3296.69
7	63.40	1231.50	196.12	169.94	79.16	352.49
8	39.97	422.04	127.16	38.78	0.47	132.65
9	128.51	1889.80	499.26	235.06	5.30	692.98
10	272.62	2928.29	698.92	324.88	6.65	1023.16
11	463.32	635.69	1210.83	746.99	82.72	1919.40
12	431.01	2642.87	487.81	1204.86	16.97	1729.50
13	2124.89	18324.41	5067.49	6140.76	217.24	10392.72
14	234.11	4582.91	1366.33	1711.10	8.02	3218.60
15	63.06	1129.94	127.44	656.02	53.23	830.51
16	42.45	202.12	137.71	31.53	0.00	153.20
Total	8238.64	109109.65	25919.12	20071.93	635.78	45541.78

Table 4.32. Indirect Effects of the Industry Depending on the Port (1998)-Choice 2

Sectors	Employment	Sales	Wages	GES	Taxes	GAV
1	128.83	560.21	33.18	222.89	0.30	229.04
2	368.47	10669.16	2080.75	2562.42	27.27	5231.91
3	1063.91	21578.67	4077.58	2656.19	25.99	6652.42
4	159.95	4906.65	696.58	495.54	5.60	1227.13
5	1915.17	23398.44	6198.89	2541.60	32.04	8709.85
6	793.26	15049.20	3124.60	458.30	78.19	3392.61
7	64.96	1261.74	200.94	174.11	81.11	361.15
8	40.37	426.28	128.44	39.16	0.48	133.98
9	132.28	1945.27	513.91	241.96	5.46	713.33
10	284.78	3058.99	730.11	339.38	6.94	1068.83
11	489.47	671.57	1279.17	789.15	87.39	2027.73
12	444.35	2724.64	502.91	1242.14	17.50	1783.01
13	2272.19	19594.63	5418.76	6566.43	232.30	11113.13
14	245.95	4814.81	1435.46	1797.68	8.42	3381.47
15	67.94	1217.35	137.30	706.77	57.35	894.76
16	44.03	209.66	142.85	32.70	0.00	158.91
Total	8515.91	112087.26	26701.44	20866.45	666.32	47079.24

Table 4.33. Induced Effects of the Industry Depending on the Port (1998)-Choice 1

Sectors	Employment	Sales	Wages	GES	Taxes	GAV
1	1924.35	8367.75	495.60	3329.33	4.52	3421.16
2	140.74	4075.26	794.78	978.76	10.41	1998.41
3	106.50	2160.02	408.17	265.88	2.60	665.91
4	172.81	5301.20	752.60	535.39	6.05	1325.80
5	217.39	2655.89	703.62	288.49	3.64	988.63
6	150.19	2849.26	591.58	86.77	14.80	642.32
7	1414.80	27481.29	4376.51	3792.19	1766.56	7865.94
8	292.80	3092.06	931.65	284.08	3.46	971.84
9	117.27	1724.57	455.61	214.50	4.84	632.40
10	258.57	2777.44	662.91	308.15	6.30	970.45
11	237.41	325.74	620.45	382.77	42.39	983.53
12	3758.81	23048.23	4254.18	10507.52	148.01	15082.82
13	617.65	5326.42	1472.99	1784.96	63.15	3020.89
14	394.78	7728.26	2304.07	2885.47	13.52	5427.60
15	216.55	3880.22	437.64	2252.79	182.80	2851.98
16	867.66	4131.03	2814.67	644.40	0.00	3131.17
Total	**10888.29**	**104924.63**	**22077.01**	**28541.43**	**2273.03**	**49980.85**

Table 4.34. Induced Effects of the Industry Depending on the Port (1998)-Choice 2

Sectors	Employment	Sales	Wages	GES	Taxes	GAV
1	1941.11	8440.61	499.92	3358.32	4.55	3450.95
2	141.97	4110.75	801.70	987.28	10.51	2015.81
3	107.43	2178.83	411.72	268.20	2.62	671.71
4	174.32	5347.36	759.15	540.05	6.10	1337.35
5	219.28	2679.02	709.75	291.00	3.67	997.24
6	151.50	2874.07	596.73	87.53	14.93	647.92
7	1427.12	27720.60	4414.62	3825.21	1781.94	7934.44
8	295.35	3118.98	939.76	286.56	3.49	980.31
9	118.29	1739.59	459.57	216.37	4.88	637.90
10	260.82	2801.62	668.69	310.83	6.36	978.90
11	239.48	328.57	625.85	386.10	42.75	992.09
12	3791.54	23248.93	4291.23	10599.02	149.30	15214.16
13	623.03	5372.80	1485.81	1800.50	63.70	3047.19
14	398.22	7795.55	2324.13	2910.60	13.64	5474.86
15	218.43	3914.01	441.45	2272.40	184.39	2876.81
16	875.21	4167.00	2839.18	650.01	0.00	3158.44
Total	10983.10	**105838.32**	**22269.26**	**28789.97**	**2292.83**	**50416.08**

4.2.6 Total Effects of the Industry Depending on the Port

Once the direct, indirect and induced effects of the Industry Depending on the Port have been estimated, we will proceed to add the different effects for the two choices in order to obtain Tables 4.35 and 4.36.

Here we must point out that the results obtained for any of both choices are remarkably better than those attained for 1993. Employment has increased in absolute terms between 18.5% and 20%; the GAV has grown between 58.1 and 60% and the remaining variables show a highly positive behavior, except for taxes whose collection has decreased between 6.7% and 7.5%. This improvement has also been appreciated in relative terms. Thus, in 1993 the Industry Depending on the Port accounted for 14.7% of employment in Cantabria while in 1998, it represented around 17.3 % of such employment. On the other hand, the Industry Depending on the Port accounted for about 16.1% of the GAV in 1993 while it represented 21.57% of the GAV in 1998.

Table 4.35. Total Effects. Industry Depending on the Port-Choice 1

	Employment	Sales	Wages	GES	Taxes	GAV
Total Direct	10889.2	401789.8	63919.7	59351.5	3567.2	123271.1
Total Indirect	8238.64	109109.65	25919.12	20071.93	635.78	45541.78
Total Induced	10888.3	104924.6	22077.0	28541.4	2273.0	49980.8
Total 1998	30016.1	615824.0	111915.8	107964.9	6476.0	218793.7
Total 1993	25334.0	306255.4	66907.2	51832.7	6027.8	118740.0
Total 1993 (pesetas 1998)	25334.0	355562.5	77679.3	60177.8	6998.3	137857.1
Variation (%)	18.5	73.2	44.1	79.4	-7.5	58.7

Table 4.36. Total Effects. Industry Depending on the Port-Choice 2

	Employment	Sales	Wages	GES	Taxes	GAV
Total Direct	10889.2	401789.8	63919.7	59351.5	3567.2	123271.1
Total Indirect	8515.91	112087.26	26701.44	20866.45	666.32	47079.24
Total Induced	10983.1	105838.3	22269.3	28790.0	2292.8	50416.1
Total 1998	30388.2	619715.3	112890.3	109007.9	6526.3	220766.4
Total 1993	25334.0	306255.4	66907.2	51832.7	6027.8	118740.0
Total 1993 (pesetas 1998)	25334.0	355562.5	77679.3	60177.8	6998.3	137857.1
Variation (%)	20.0	74.3	45.3	81.1	-6.7	60.1

4.2.7 Economic Impact Study

Tables 4.37 and 4.38 present the aggregation of the results for Port Industry and the Industry Depending on the Port.

The results for 1993 gave relative values for employment between 16.1 and 16.8% of the total of regional employment using the same methodology, while for the

GAV, total impact values were between 17.5 and 18.2 % of the total regional
GAV. The total impact values now presented have increased in relative terms in a
range between 19.16 and 19.38% for employment and between 23.35 and 23.5%
for the regional GAV. This growth is approximately three points for regional
employment, which means an increase of over 5,000 jobs as compared with 1993
and about five points for the GAV, over 50,000 million pesetas more with respect
to 1998. This implies that the growth of Port Industry and the Industry Depending
on the Port - in other words, the economic impact of the Port –has exceeded the
regional economy growth with 5,000 jobs and 50,000 million pesetas. The port is
revealed not only as an important economic impact on the region but also as the
driving force of regional economy as far as its good working and own growth
movement increasingly lead to a more positive development in Cantabria.

Table 4.37. Total Effects-Choice 1

	Employment	Sales	Wages	GES	Taxes	GAV
Total Direct	12348.2	431825.0	71939.2	63526.6	29175.4	135465.7
Total Indirect	9301.5	119681.4	29160.6	22980.8	898.8	51675.0
Total Induced	11301.8	108926.4	22918.3	29622.0	2449.1	51877.9
Total 1998	32951.4	660432.9	124018.2	116129.4	32523.3	239018.6
Total 1993	28935.0	339604.4	75465.0	59063.6	17236.0	134571.1
Total 1993 (pesetas 1998)	28935.0	394280.7	87614.9	68572.8	20011.0	156237.0
		67.50322				
Variation (%)	13.8808712	71	41.5492241	69.3518459	62.5271161	52.9845859

Table 4.38. Total Effects-Choice 2

	Employment	Sales	Wages	GES	Taxes	GAV
Total Direct	12348.2	431825.0	71939.2	63526.6	29175.4	135465.7
Total Indirect	9578.8	122659.0	29942.9	23775.3	929.3	53212.4
Total Induced	11396.6	109840.1	23110.6	29870.5	2468.9	52313.2
Total 1998	33323.5	664324.2	124992.7	117172.4	32573.6	240991.3
Total 1993	28935.0	339604.4	75465.0	59063.6	17236.0	134571.1
Total 1993 (pesetas 1998)	28935.0	394280.7	87614.9	68572.8	20011.0	156237.0
		68.490164				
Variation (%)	15.1668341	1	42.6615568	70.87293	62.778631	54.2472191

4.3 Final Remarks

Through the computable GE models such as the Leontief model we can obtain very useful applications for the economy in order to find the impact of a firm, a sector, a port, an airport, etc., on the economy. Only by using GE models it is possible to estimate all the effects. At present, some interesting applications are being developed in the environmental field from computable general equilibrium estimations which use SAM databases (Matrix of Social Accounts).

Bibliographic References

Coto-Millán, P., Gallego, J. L., Villaverde, J.: Crecimiento y Desarrollo Portuario. Aplicación al Puerto de Santander. Autoridad Portuaria de Santander 2001

Villaverde, J., Coto-Millán, P.: El impacto económico del Puerto de Santander en la economía cántabra. Autoridad Portuaria de Santander 1995

Villaverde, J., Coto-Millán, P.: Impacto económico portuario: Metodologías para su análisis y aplicación al Puerto de Santander. 1996

Villaverde, J., Coto-Millán, P.: Port Economic Impact: methodologies and appliation to the Port of Santander. International Journal of Transport Economics. Special Issue: Infrastructure Investment and Development Vol. XXV-N. 2, 159-179 (1998)

Villaverde, J., Coto-Millán, P.: Guest Editor's Introduction. International Journal of Transport Economics. Special Issue: Infrastructure Investment and Development Vol. XXV-N. 2, 109-112 (1998)

5 Welfare

5.1
Positive Properties of the GE Model

After two centuries of advances, the general equilibrium theory has developed an acceptable model as regards inner consistency and capacity of prediction. Which desired properties does this model present? Its allocations are:

i) Physically feasible
ii) Technically and allocatively efficient
iii) Unbiased quality

All these are desired properties. A non-feasible allocation would require more resources than those available and would be unattainable since it would need to create productive resources from nothing.

Efficiency is a desired property. If it is not satisfied greater quantities of some goods could be produced without reducing the production of others or some people's welfare could be improved without affecting others' welfare. Its unbiased quality means that any optimal state in a Pareto sense may be achieved through competitive mechanism. Although the properties of feasibility, efficiency and unbiased quality are desired, they are very weak.

Feasibility only indicates that the restrictions of the individual optimization problems of each agent are satisfied.

Efficiency is conditioned to an exogenous distribution of the wealth. This is a key question. The resource assignments from the individuals (capital and labor) are significant data since each individual's wealth will result from multiplying such assignment by the equilibrium prices of capital and labor. Prices only guarantee technical, economic or global efficiency conditions such that the distribution of the resulting wealth in the model is not related with considerations about equity or commutative fairness but it is given by history.

Finally, unbiased quality indicates that, for all state of the economy that is Pareto optimum, there is an initial distribution of wealth from which such state can be achieved. However, nothing is mentioned about how to achieve the optimum distribution.

5.2
The First Welfare Theorem

The solution found for the Walrasian GE Model (extended by Arrow-Debreu) is Pareto-efficient, in other words, competitive equilibrium is Pareto Optimum.

5.3
The Second Welfare Theorem

All Pareto-efficient state may be achieved from a Walrasian GE Model (extended by Arrow-Debreu). With each specific resource assignment from the consumers and a productive technology it is possible to obtain a wide range of Pareto Optimums in relation with the initial assignments from the agents. Any Pareto Optimum we desire may be achieved from a GE Model whenever the initial resource assignment can be properly distributed among the agents of production.

Important: the two previous theorems are not reciprocal. The first theorem proves the existence of efficiency while the second theorem proves that the system of prices is unbiased.

The second theorem widely justifies direct taxes since the initial assignment is modified, allowing the price system to achieve its Pareto-efficient equilibrium.

We will highlight more aspects about the second Theorem of Welfare. Under some specific conditions, all the efficient allocations in the Pareto sense can be attained by means of the mechanism of competitive equilibrium. In other words, the market mechanism allows us to obtain any efficient allocation in the desired Pareto sense. This means that any distribution which we consider as "fair" or "good" for collective welfare can be attained by using competitive markets. In line with this, in general, is it necessary to re-distribute assignments among consumers. In particular, it is necessary to re-distribute both the income generated from labor assignments and the shares held in the company. This may seem simple but can present big problems from the practical point of view.

Starting from A (OP) in order to achieve C, we will have to take part of x from individual B $[x^B_1 - x^B_0]$ and provide individual A$[x^A_1 - x^A_0]$ with that part of x, and then, take part of y from individual B$[y^B_1 - y^B_0]$ and provide A$[y^B_1 - y^B_0]$ with that part of y.

It is difficult to assume a real economy which is only based on tax and transference systems which impose charges or distribute premiums in different quantities notwithstanding the market activities of the agents. The first theorem establishes a presumption which supports the competitive mechanism. The first theorem does not deal with Equity at all, as sometimes remarked, however, the second theorem states that, if we wish to attain a specific distribution of the economic system, there is not any logic need to sacrifice Pareto-sense efficiency in the allocation of resources. If an "adequate" – or at least apparently adequate – policy of re-distribution is adopted, it will be possible to obtain an optimal allocation of resources in the Pareto sense and preserve equity at the same time, based on competitive markets.

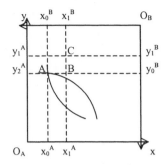

Fig. 5.1

5.4
Compensation Criteria

By compensation criteria we mean the criteria aimed at compensating some agents when their welfare is affected by the welfare attained by other agents. For example, a village in a valley is flooded to increase the water supply of other villages. Here it would be necessary for beneficiaries to compensate damaged people under certain criteria. A first criterion would be that the growth of the welfare generated for the agents as a result of any type of action is higher than the damages generated to the agents who lose welfare as a consequence of such an action. A second criterion is that an action can be executed when the individuals damaged by it can be compensated by the beneficiaries of such an action until they reach their initial state of welfare. Unfortunately, there are some cases in which both criteria are simultaneously satisfied, a fact which weakens the compensation criteria.

For an Edgeworth's box such as:

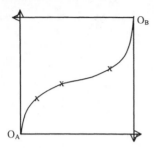

Fig. 5.2

The utility possibilities curve will be:

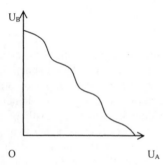

Fig. 5.3

Which indicates that, as we move from O_B to O_A utility u_A grows and u_B goes down. Thus, with these tools we can say that a specific action – suppression of a monopoly , flood of a village, etc. – will produce the shift of the utility possibilities frontier or curve, for example, towards the right.

In other words,

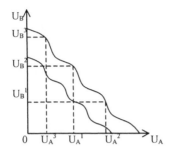

Fig. 5.4

Starting now from the initial situation $\{u_A{}^1, u_B{}^1\}$ the action may lead us to obtain either combination $\{u_A{}^2, u_B{}^1\}$ or combination $\{u_B{}^2, u_A{}^1\}$, any of these situations being higher in the Pareto sense. However, what would happen if we had combination $\{u_A{}^3, u_B{}^3\}$? In this case A would enjoy lower welfare than the initial one while B would have higher welfare. Therefore, B could always compensate A by transferring utility units to this individual until situation $\{u_A{}^1, u_B{}^2\}$ was achieved, where A is at the initial state and B is at a better state of welfare than at the beginning. However, some doubts may exist given that changing from $\{u_A{}^1, u_B{}^1\}$ to $\{u_A{}^3, u_B{}^3\}$ implies a Pareto improvement but changing from $\{u_A{}^3, u_B{}^3\}$ to $\{u_A{}^2, u_B{}^2\}$ is not guaranteed unless B is compelled to compensate A, otherwise, only the possibility would exist.

Moreover, there may be contradictory results for the two above-mentioned compensation criteria. Assuming possibility frontiers of initial and final utility such as u_1, u_2 and representing them as in figure 5.5:
The initial situation will be now $\{u_A{}^1, u_B{}^1\}$ while the final situation will be $\{u_A{}^2, u_B{}^2\}$. In this case, individual B, in view of the losses of individual A, can offer the latter utility units so that A may return to the initial situation, that is to say, until this individual achieves combination $\{u_B{}^3, u_A{}^1\}$. On the other hand, from situation $\{u_A{}^2, u_B{}^2\}$, individual A may also offer B utility units so that this individual achieves situation $\{u_A{}^3, u_B{}^2\}$ where A gains $\{u_A{}^3 - u_A{}^2\}$ and B keeps the same utility $u_B{}^3$. In this way, both compensation criteria are simultaneously satisfied they becoming contradictory and useless.

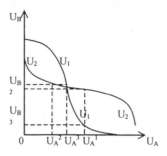

Fig. 5.5

5.5
The Theory of the "Second Best"

In Competitive General Equilibrium the fact that optimality conditions stop being satisfied for a firm or sector will generally lead to a different economy. For this reason, the rest of companies and sectors must not continue keeping their optimality conditions as if such perturbation did not exist; they must modify those conditions. In other words, all the results must be altered.

Determining the efficient allocation conditions when any of those first best conditions is not satisfied is called "second best problem".

The problem is that this second best condition is not susceptible of being dealt with from a general point of view as in the case of the first best. In view of this, we can only study specific cases and find solutions for the second best. For example, being an economy with a private monopoly which produces good x_1, assume now that the Public Administration tries to correct the perturbation generated by the existence of monopoly by creating a public company which produces good x_2, close substitute for x_1. The aim of this public firm will be to maximize the global surplus of society, which, in partial equilibrium conditions will be:

$$E\,(x_1, x_2) = \int_0^{x_1} P_1(x_1, x_2)dx_1 + \int_0^{x_2} P_2(x_1, x_2)dx_2 - C_1(x_1) - C_2(x_2)$$

The public firm will estimate a reaction function of the private firm when it starts to produce, which we will express as:

$$x_1 = \psi\,(x_2)$$

In other words, the public firm will take into account the demand for good x_1 and expectations with respect to the private monopolist behavior.

Maximization of $E\,(x_1, x_2)$ requires that:

$$d\,E(x_1, x_2) = (P_1 - C'_1\,(x_1))\,dx_1 + (P_2 - C'_2\,(x_2))\,dx_2 = 0$$

from which

$$P_2 - C'_2 (x_2) = (P_1 - C'_1 (x_1)) \, dx_1/dx_2; \text{ con } dx_1/dx_2 = \psi' (x_2)$$

In other words, the public firm must not behave either competitively or as a competitive company and it must not follow the rule: price equals marginal cost.

If x_1 is produced in monopoly $P_1 > C'_1 (x_1)$ and since x_2 is substitute for x_1, it is expected that dx_1/dx_2 - conjectural variation – has a positive sign. Therefore, the following can be guaranteed:

$$- (P_1 - C'_1 (x_1)) \, dx_1/dx_2 > 0$$

However, with the aim that dx_1/dx_2 has a negative sign, it must be broken into:

$$dx_1/dx_2 = (dx_1/dP_2) \cdot \quad (dP_2/dx_2)$$

Since x_2 is a substitute for x_1 then $(dx_1/dP_2) > 0$ and, for normal goods $(dP_2/dx_2) < 0$ therefore, we can expect $(dx_1/dx_2) < 0$.

If $[- (P_1 - C'_1 (x_1)) \, dx_1/dx_2 > 0]$ with $[(dx_1/dx_2) < 0]$, now it is necessary that:

$$P_2 > C'_2 (x_2) \text{ ó } P_2 - C'_2 (x_2) > 0$$

With this we are stating that the public firm must fix a cost higher than the marginal cost.

In short, the theory of the second best guarantees that between two states of the economy which are non-optimal in Pareto sense, if one is not higher than the other, there is not a pattern to measure the desirability of one with respect to the other. This does not mean that any partial attempt to satisfy the optimality conditions in the Pareto sense is vain but that this kind of attempts must be focused in practice on eliminating the least desirable states. Although the analyses of welfare economy are partial we must not waive them. In fact, they seem to show increasingly more utility[1].

5.6
Problems of the GE Model

There are many efficient allocations, each one implying a different wealth distribution on which the system cannot exert any effect.

1st Problem. The model lacks any desired property with respect to income and wealth distribution in society.

Does this mean that the economic theory is not capable of considering income distribution? No, it doesn't. The Theory of Social Choice, a branch of the economic analysis, which is an intersection between Economy, Logic and Ethics; has achieved important advances on the collective assessment of resource allocations since its initial stage in the works by (1938) and Arrow (1951), which enables us to formulate thoroughly, in terms of the logical content of the economic analysis, ethical criteria to define equal and envy-free allocations as well as

---

[1] See Ky Lipsey, R.G. (1956-57). "The General Theory of second best". Review Economic Studies, 24, 11-32.

establishing interpersonal comparisons of utility and defining individual rights. The works of Sen (1970, 1986) are essential in these fields.

2nd Problem. In competitive economies there are two assumptions with a key role:

i) Individuals consider prices as given. (Parametric behavior of agents with respect to prices).
ii) Only prices give all the necessary information for the individuals to take their decisions.

What happens if this circumstance does not occur? If individual agents do not take prices as given, they may influence said prices, for example, a monopolist may freely determine the sale prices of his goods or a group of companies may act strategically. The natural way of analysis of the strategic behavior of agents supports on the Games Theory initiated by Morgenstern and von Newmann (1947) and its systematic study has been included in another branch of the economic analysis called Industrial Economy [for instance, Tirole (1988) and Wiliamson (1990)].

From these analyses we infer that, in view of the strategic behaviors, the competitive equilibrium loses its essential desirable property: being an efficient resource allocation. This gives rise to a branch of the economic policy called policy for the defense of competition.

What happens if prices do not provide all the relevant and unique information? We would have what is called market failures. For instance, when ones' actions affect the others' possibilities there exist external effects. For example, when information is asymmetrically distributed among the agents (when we buy a second-hand car or when we go to the doctor's we always have less information than the car seller or the doctor about the goods: the car or our health) equilibrium is not Efficient either and the final price is higher and the quality of the goods or service lower than the optimum.

The existence of market failures has led to the development of another recent branch of analysis: the Theory of Regulation [Spulber (1985)], which tries to determine the way in which the action of agents on markets may be restricted so that they allocate resources efficiently. In other words, once the problem has been described, we must propose regulation as a type of action which may correct the behavior of agents in order to achieve the desired objectives. Can we describe a regulation mechanism or is it better to let the market act? This fact will depend on each specific situation.

5.6.1 Problems of Property Rights Allocation

5.6.1.1 Public Goods

Public goods are those goods whose consumption or use of one unit by an individual does not reduce at all its consumption and use by other individuals. Therefore, public goods are non-rival and non-excluding with respect consumption or use by other individuals. For example, social security, public lighting and law administration are public goods generally provided by the State. Moreover, a TV set for two room mates is a public good as both of them can watch it when it is turned on. For this case we aim at providing some rules for behavior with respect to the private supply of the public good (TV set) to the individuals of a society (room mates).

The first rule is that the cost of acquisition of the public good must be always lower than or equal to the quantitythe individuals who are willing to pay for its supply.

The second rule is that although the first rule is satisfied, it is possible that a public good is not approximated by individuals. In other words, it may happen that individuals do not agree on buying a public good in spite of the first rule being satisfied and whether the good is supplied or not will depend on the method adopted by the individuals to take the decision.

The third rule implies that, when individuals sincerely reveal the subjective value that the public good has to them, agreement will be easy and the good will be probably supplied. When individuals hide their personal reasons to get the good they develop free-rider behaviors.

In order to illustrate the above rules we assume A and B as individuals of an economy and the utility represented by the supply of the public good to each individual is 30 monetary units. The total cost of the supply of the public good is 40 monetary units and the wealth of each individual is 50 units before acquiring the public goods.

The game can be exposed as:

		Player B			
		Buying		Not buying	
Player A	Buying	60	60	40	80
	Not buying	80	40	50	50

In other words, if A and B decide to buy and pay the public good at 50%, each one will pay 20 monetary units and receive a utility of 30 monetary units each in addition to 30 monetary units of initial assignment which they have still available. On the other hand, if A buys and B doesn't, A will pay 40 and receive a utility of 30 plus 10 monetary units of initial assignment he still has. Meanwhile, B acts as a free-rider as he receives 30 monetary units of utility for watching TV without any cost, which, in addition to the 50 units he had, quantityto 80 utility units.

The remaining boxes of the game matrix could be explained in similar terms. Note that only in those situations where the utility of a public good for an individual is higher than its cost the supply of said public good is always guaranteed, while in other cases such supply is not guaranteed. Moreover, even in those cases where supply is guaranteed, the cost of the public good does not behave efficiently since one individual pays the whole cost of it and the other enjoys the good free. In those cases when two individuals exist we have observed that only co-operation and sincere display of their preferences and values may lead to efficient solutions of the problem. As the number of individuals increases the situation becomes more complex since there are more potential free-riders.

5.6.1.1.1 Model with 2 Consumers and 1 Exogenous Public Good

In terms of a continuous public good in general equilibrium, the problem may be formulated as follows. Being an economy formed by two consumers A and B and being BP the public good, the initial assignment of wealth of each individual is w_A and w_B and the private good is x_i. If we wish to know the optimal allocations of BP for each individual, we will pose the optimization problem as:

$$\max U_A(x_A, BP)$$

$$x_A, x_B, BP$$

$$\text{s. to} \quad U_B(x_B, BP) = \overline{U}_B$$

$$x_A + x_B + c(BP) = w_a + w_B$$

where $c(BP)$ is the cost of the public good BP.

$$L = U_A(x_A, BP) - \lambda[U_B(x_B, BP) - \overline{U}_B]$$

$$- \mu[x_A + x_B + c(BP) - w_A - w_B]$$

The first order conditions require that:

$$\frac{\partial L}{\partial x_A} = \frac{\partial U_A(x_A, BP)}{\partial x_A} - \mu = 0$$

$$\frac{\partial L}{\partial x_B} = -\lambda \frac{\partial U_B(x_B, BP)}{\partial x_B} - \mu = 0$$

$$\frac{\partial L}{\partial BP} = \frac{\partial U_A(x_A, BP)}{\partial BP} - \lambda \frac{\partial U_B(x_B, BP)}{\partial BP} - \mu \frac{\partial c(BP)}{\partial BP} = 0$$

By dividing the last derivative by μ and reordering terms, we obtain:

$$\frac{1}{\mu} \frac{\partial U_A(x_A, BP)}{\partial BP} - \frac{\lambda}{\mu} \frac{\partial U_B(x_B, BP)}{\partial BP} = \frac{\partial c(BP)}{\partial BP}$$

Finding μ in the first derivative we obtain:

$$\mu = \frac{\partial U_A(x_A, BP)}{\partial BP}$$

Finding μ/λ in the second derivative we obtain:

$$\frac{\mu}{\lambda} = -\frac{\partial U_B(x_B, BP)}{\partial BP}$$

Now we substitute the last two statements on the one which appears previous to them and we obtain:

$$\frac{\partial U_A(x_A, BP)}{\partial BP} / \frac{\partial U_A(x_A, BP)}{\partial x_A} + \frac{\partial U_B(x_B, BP)}{\partial BP} / \frac{\partial U_B(x_B, BP)}{\partial x_B} = \frac{\partial c(BP)}{\partial BP}$$

In other words:

$$MRS_A + MRS_B = MC(BP)$$

This implies that the addition of the marginal rates of substitution between the private and the public good must be equal to the marginal cost of supplying an additional unit of the public good.

Graphically:

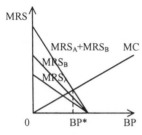

Fig. 5.6

Where BP* will be the optimum quantity of the public good BP to be supplied.

5.6.1.1.2 Model with 2 Consumers and 1 Endogenous Public Good

In order to give more realism to the problem, we will assume now the above example for a company which produces public good BP by means of private good x_i where i= 1,2,...n, in other words, with n consumers. In this case, the optimization problem would be the following:

$$\max \Sigma_i \alpha_i U_i(x_i, BP); \alpha_i > 0$$

$$x_i, BP$$

s. to $x_i + \theta = w$

$$BP = BP(\theta)$$

Where θ represents the quantityof private good x employed as input to produce public good BP and where BP = BP (θ) is the productive technology of the public good with $dBP/d\theta > 0$ and $d^2BP/d\theta^2 < 0$.

The intermediate Lagrange function is:

$$L = \Sigma_i \alpha_i U_i (x_i, BP) - \lambda [x_i + \theta - w] - \mu [BP - BP(\theta)]$$

The first order conditions are now:

$$\frac{\partial L}{\partial x_i} = \alpha_i \frac{\partial U_i}{\partial x_i} - \lambda = 0$$

$$\frac{\partial L}{\partial BP} = \sum_{i=1}^{n} \alpha_i \frac{\partial U_i}{\partial BP} - \mu = 0$$

$$\frac{\partial L}{\partial \theta} = -\lambda + \mu \frac{dBP(\theta)}{d\theta} = 0$$

From where, by substituting the value of μ in the second derivative and the value of λ in the first derivative, in the third one we obtain:

$$\alpha_i \frac{\partial U_i}{\partial x_i} + \sum_{i=1}^{n} \alpha_i \frac{\partial U_i}{\partial BP} \frac{dBP(\theta)}{d\theta} = 0$$

By replacing α_i with its value $\lambda/(\partial U_i/\partial x_i)$ we obtain:

$$\frac{\lambda}{\partial U_i / \partial x_i} \frac{\partial U_i}{\partial x_i} + \sum_{i=1}^{n} \frac{\lambda}{\partial U_i / \partial x_i} \frac{\partial U_i}{\partial BP} \frac{dBP(\theta)}{d\theta} = 0$$

$$\lambda = \lambda \sum_{i=1}^{n} \frac{\partial U_i / \partial BP}{\partial U_i / \partial x_i} \frac{dBP(\theta)}{d\theta}$$

in other words

$$\frac{1}{dBP(\theta)/d\theta} = \sum_{i=1}^{n} \frac{\partial U_i / \partial BP}{\partial U_i / \partial x_i} = MRS_{x_i}^{BP}$$

which is the Bowen-Lindahl-Samuelson condition (Laffont, 1982) for optimality: "the addition of the marginal rates of substitution between the public good and the private good must equal the marginal rate of transformation between the public good and the private good ". Obviously:

$$dx_i(x_i)/dx_i = 1$$

5.6.1.1.3 Model with L Consumers and 1 Endogenous Public Good

If the economy operates privately and individuals finance the production of public good BP by popular decision, each one contributing with a quantity θ_i of resources depending on their preferences, the production of the public good will be:

$$BP = BP(\Sigma_i \theta_i)$$

and the optimization problem will be for the i-th individual:

$$\max U_i (x_i, BP)$$

$$x_i, BP$$

s. to $x_i + \theta_i = w_i$

$$BP = BP(\theta_i + \sum_{j \neq i} \overline{\theta}_j)$$

The contributions decided by the other consumers being

$$\sum_{j \neq i} \overline{\theta}_j .$$

therefore, the Lagrangian will be:

$$L = U_i (x_i, BP) - \lambda (x_i - w_i - \theta_i) - \mu [BP - BP(\theta_i + \sum_{j \neq i} \overline{\theta}_j)]$$

From where the first order conditions will lead to the new equilibrium condition:

$$\frac{1}{dBP(\theta) / d\theta_i} = \frac{\partial U_i / \partial BP}{\partial U_i / \partial x_i} ; i = 1, 2, ..., n$$

This statement, although similar, is not equal to that obtained in the Bowen-Lindahl-Samuelson condition since each individual only computes his own profit rather than the profit obtained for other individuals from his contribution. This implies that the private supply of a public good is lower than the optimum or efficient supply. If we were dealing with a public harm we would have the opposite result: a surplus of it. In other words, the private supply of a public good is a non co-operative game with a Nash equilibrium providing an quantityof public goods lower than the optimum amount.

In order to solve this problem we may assume that the public Administration acts either by directly providing the public goods or, alternatively, by creating new markets, as in the case of the externalities.

5.6.1.1.4 Model with L Consumers and 1 Endogenous Public Good

Assuming that each i-consumer is willing to pay a price P_i for the public good BP, the problem of the optimum would be now:

$$\max U_i (x_i, BP)$$

s. to $x_i + P_i BP = w_i$

$L = U_i (x_i, BP) - \lambda (x_i + P_i BP - w_i)$

$$\frac{\partial L}{\partial x_i} = \frac{\partial U_i}{\partial x_i} - \lambda = 0$$

$$\frac{\partial L}{\partial BP} = \frac{\partial U_i}{\partial BP} - \lambda P_i = 0$$

from where

$$\frac{\partial U_i}{\partial x_i} P_i = \frac{\partial U_i}{\partial BP}; \frac{\partial U_i / \partial x_i}{\partial U_i / \partial BP} = P_i .$$

The optimum quantity according to P_i and w_i is the Marshallian demand function of the public good BP.

Assume now that there is a private firm which produces public good BP with inputs x_i as private goods acquired from the individuals.

The price of the public good BP will be $P = \Sigma_i P_i$. In other words, it is the addition of the individual prices.

The firm which produces that public good faces the following problem:

max $(\Sigma_i P_i)BP - \theta = 0$

s. to $BP = BP(\theta)$

The intermediate Lagrange function will be:

$L = [(\Sigma_i P_i)BP - \theta] - \mu [BP - BP(\theta)]$

the first order conditions will be:

$$\frac{\partial L}{\partial BP} = \sum_{i=1}^{n} P_i - \mu = 0$$

$$\frac{\partial L}{\partial \theta} = -1 + \mu \frac{\partial BP}{\partial \theta}$$

from where

$\Sigma_i P_i = \mu = 1 / (dBP/d\theta)$

these prices are "Lindahl prices" and they are such that they satisfy the following condition:

$$\frac{1}{\partial BP / \partial \theta} = \frac{\partial U_i / \partial BP}{\partial U_i / \partial x_i},$$

in other words, these prices provide efficient allocations.

The prices may also be interpreted as if they were tax rates. If BP* units of the public good are supplied, individual i will have to pay a tax rate p_i BP. For this reason, Lindahl prices are sometimes called Lindahl taxes.

5.6.1.2. Natural Resources

5.6.1.2.1 Renewable Natural Resources and the Problem of Extinction of Species

There are renewable natural resources such as fish, forests and land in contrast with non-renewable natural resources such as cardboard and oil. The difference between the former and the latter group is that renewable resources can be regularly exploited while non-renewable resources constitute a "world stock" which is gradually running out. However, if renewable resources are not rationally exploited they may also run out. This is the case of the extinction of some species as well as of the irreversible deterioration of natural environment (forests and land).

On the whole, renewable resources are those which undergo a natural growth until they reach a stationary equilibrium. In line with this, we can represent graphically the fishing resources of an area as follows:

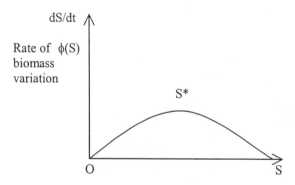

Fig. 5.7

In this figure, dS/dt represents the growth of the stock of fish resources per time unit; S is the quantity of stock of fish resources and S* represents the stationary equilibrium, in other words, the maximum fishing population that will ever exist without human participation, also called natural equilibrium. The curve represents a quite usual growth of fish population. When this population is low there is a more efficient use of resources, which accelerates fish growth (there is not scarcity of food); when population increases the resources become scarce (there is scarcity of food) and fish growth decelerates until a level S* is reached, which is the maximum stock of population the ocean is capable of sustaining

Introducing now the Fishing activity (human participation) as a capture function:

$$C = C\ (E,\ S)$$

where C is the volume of captures, E is the fishing effort (a vector of inputs such as labor and equipment) and S is the stock of fish resources. Then, the population equilibrium is obtained when it is verified that:

$$C = dS/dt$$

This means that there is equilibrium stock if:

$$C = (E,\ S) = \phi\ (S)$$

where $\phi\ (S) > 0$, for all $0 < S < S^*$; $\phi\ (0) = \phi\ (S) = 0$ and where $\phi''\ (S) \leq 0$. Graphically:

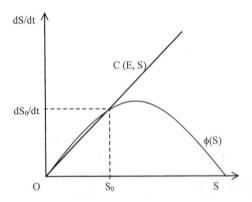

Fig. 5.8

Assuming now that the fishing effort may increase successively for values E_0, E_1 and E_2 a paradoxical situation such as that described in the following figure may occur:

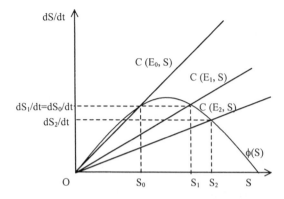

Fig. 5.9

Where we can observe that when the effort exceeds a certain limit of captures (dS/dt) start to decrease. In fact, with effort E_1 the level of captures generated is the same as with effort E_0,

On the other hand, since:

$$dS/dt = C = C (E, S)$$

it will always be possible to express S (biomass stock) as an effort function:

$$S = S (E)$$

and therefore:

$$C = C (S (E), E) = \psi (E)$$

This last functional statement can be represented in the following figure as:

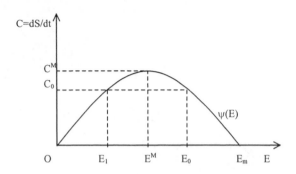

Fig. 5.10

where $\psi(E)$ is the curve of sustainable returns, E^M is the maximum sustainable return G^M and, for higher or lower efforts than E^M, the sustainable level of captures is below C^M.

In order to expose the economic equilibrium of the fishing activity the following situations are required:

i) The marginal Cost of the effort is constant.
ii) The level of captures G per unit of effort E is proportional to the amount of population.
iii) The level of captures does not affect the fish price.
iv) Fish resources are owned by either a public or a private agent.

The total Cost of capturing fish for the owner under the first assumption can be expressed a follows:

$$TC = \beta E$$

So the Marginal Cost will be constant and will have the value of β. We can now represent this Cost function in the following figure along with the curve of sustainable returns:

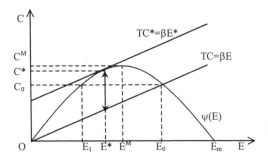

Fig. 5.11

The profit for the agent-owner of the fish resources will be:

$\pi = P \ \psi(E) - \beta \ E$

Then, he will try to maximize this profit, so the first order condition requires that:

$d\pi/dE = P \ \psi'(E) - \beta = 0$

in other words:

$P \ \psi'(E) - \beta = 0$

$P \ \psi'(E) = \beta$

that is to say, that the fishing marginal income or the marginal value $P \ \psi'(E)$ equals the fishing Marginal Cost β or alternatively, that the marginal return $\psi'(E)$ equals the relative price of the effort unit β/P. Moreover, in order to get the maximum profit the second order condition must be satisfied:

$d^2\pi/dE^2 = P \ \psi''(E) < 0$

in other words, it is required that the curve of sustainable returns is concave, which implies the existence of decreasing marginal returns.

Let's extend the assumption of one agent also assuming that there are as many agents as we wish with free access to the fish resources of the oceans.

If there is free access there will be freedom of entry in the industry and the existence of positive extraordinary profits (as we saw $\pi > 0$) will attract less agents until they disappear. This implies that long-term economic equilibrium will be produced when $\pi = 0$. In other words, when

$P \ \psi(E) = \beta \ E$

To be more simplistic, let's consider $P = 1$. Graphically:

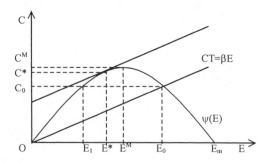

Fig. 5.12

The economic equilibrium with free competition between the agents will be achieved for the level of effort E_0, which is higher than E^* -corresponding to the effort of only one agent-owner- and also higher than E^M, which is the effort for the maximum sustainable return. From here we infer that allocation with free access is inefficient and the fish resources being owned by only one agent, either public or private, prevent both over-exploitation and the disappearance of profits. However, such a situation does not necessarily lead to the exhaustion of the resource. This situation would occur if the cost of the effort were null, then (with $CT = \beta E = 0$) we would reach the maximum level of effort E_m and the extinction of species would be produced. This would be given in static terms, in dynamic terms, if it were constantly verified that the growth rate of captures is higher than the growth rate (or reposition) of biomass, fish resources would run out.

5.6.1.2.2 A Bioeconomic Model

Populations, together with the fishing biomass, increase over time according to a logistic function or curve in S form such as the following:

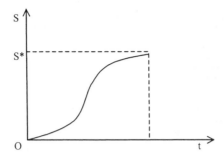

Fig. 5.13

Such a logistic gives the idea of initial slow growth when biomass is small and of exponential increases when said biomass increases. Then, such exponential increases gradually decrease as biomass increases due to environmental resistences. Quantity S* can be denominated level of natural equilibrium, representing the maximum amount of biomass which can be upheld by the environment to which population will naturally tend without human involvement.

The functional statement of a logistic which measures the increase of the fishing biomass is:

$$S = g\, S \left[\frac{S}{gS^*} - (1 - \frac{S}{S^*})e^{-gt} \right]$$

where S is the amount of fishing biomass, g is the natural or biological growth rate of the fishing population, S* is the amount of natural equilibrium biomass, A is a parameter, e is number e and t is time. By operating and deriving the above statement with respect to time t we obtain:

$$S = g\frac{S^2}{gS^*} - gSe^{-gt} + g\frac{S^2}{S^*}e^{-gt}$$

$$\frac{dS}{dt} = (-g)\left[-gSe^{-gt} + g\frac{S^2}{S^*}e^{-gt} \right]$$

$$\frac{1}{g}\frac{dS}{dt} = gSe^{-gt} - g\frac{S^2}{S^*}e^{-gt} = gSe^{-gt}(1 - \frac{S}{S^*})$$

$$\frac{S^2 g}{S^* g} + \frac{1}{g}\frac{dS}{dt} = S$$

$$\frac{1}{g}\frac{dS}{dt} = S - \frac{S^2}{S^*}$$

$$\frac{dS}{dt} = g(S - \frac{S^2}{S^*}) = gS(1 - \frac{S}{S^*})$$

From this statement we can say that:

If $S > S^*$, $dS/dt < 0$ and population decreases.

If $S < S^*$, $dS/dt > 0$ and population increases.

If $S = S^*$, $dS/dt = 0$ and population remains stable.

Thus S/dt is maximum when:

$$\frac{\dot{S}}{dS} = \frac{dS/dt}{dS} = g - \frac{2g}{S^*}S = 0$$

in other words,

$$g = \frac{2g}{S^*}S \; ; \; S = \frac{g}{2g/S^*}$$

and, by eliminating g we obtain the maximum sustainable level of captures:

$$\dot{S} = \frac{S^*}{2}$$

graphically:

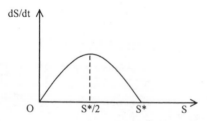

Fig. 5.14

Be now the capture function:

$$C = C \, (E, \, S)$$

where all the variables have already been previously defined.

To simplify, we assume that:

$C = \alpha\, E\, S$

where $\alpha > 0$ is a parameter.

The fish stock equilibrium will be:

$C\,(E, S) = \phi\,(S)$

in other words:

$C\,(E, S) = gS\,(1 - S/S^*)$

from where:

$\alpha ES = gS\,(1 - S/S^*)$

$\alpha E = g - (Sg/S^*)$

$Sg/S^* = g - \alpha E$

$S = (g - \alpha E) / (g/\,S^*)$

$S = S^*\,(1 - E\cdot\ \alpha/g)$

since:

$S = C / \alpha E$

it is possible to write:

$C = S^*\, \alpha E\,(1 - E\cdot\ \alpha/g)$

which implies that captures are now an effort function rather than a fish stock function, therefore, it is possible to represent them graphically:

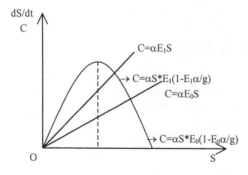

Fig. 5.15

We assume that the cost function is linear of a type which is already known:

$$CT = \beta E$$

where β is the constant marginal cost and E is the effort.

Now the profits will be the following:

$$\pi = \left[\alpha S^* E (1 - \frac{\alpha}{g} E) P - \beta E \right.$$

where P is the price of the captured fish and the amount of fish is represented by C.

In order to maximize π we must verify the first order condition:

$$\frac{d\pi}{dE} = P\alpha S^* - P\frac{2\alpha^2 S^*}{g} E - \beta = 0$$

in other words:

$$P\frac{2\alpha^2 S^*}{g} E = -\beta + P\alpha S^*$$

then:

$$E^* = \frac{g(P\alpha S^* - \beta)}{2\alpha^2 S^* P} = \frac{g}{2\alpha} - \frac{g\beta}{2P\alpha^2 S^*}$$

This is the level of effort, which corresponds to the maximum profit or equilibrium of the economy when the fish resources are owned by only one agent.

By substituting the value of E obtained in the captures or return statement we have that:

$$C = S^* \alpha E (1 - E \cdot \alpha/g)$$

then we obtain:

$$C^* = \alpha S^* \left[\frac{g(P\alpha S^* - \beta)}{2P\alpha^2 S^*} \right] \left[1 - \frac{\alpha}{g} \left(\frac{g}{2\alpha} - \frac{g\beta}{2P\alpha^2 S^*} \right) \right]$$

Which implies that the bioeconomic equilibrium for the maximum profit will be a level of captures C*. Again, we will extend the assumption of only one agent and allow free access to other agents.

In this case, profits must be null in the long term:

$$\pi = \left[\alpha S^* E (1 - \frac{\alpha}{g} E) \right] P - \beta E = 0$$

and due to the fact that:

$$P\alpha S^* E\left(1 - \frac{\alpha}{g} E\right) = P\alpha S^* E - \frac{P\alpha^2 S^* E^2}{g}$$

$$-\frac{P\alpha^2 S^* E^2}{g} + (P\alpha S^* - \beta)E = 0$$

$$\frac{P\alpha^2 S^* E}{g} = P\alpha S^* - \beta$$

$$E = \frac{(P\alpha S^* - \beta)g}{P\alpha^2 S^*} = \frac{g}{\alpha} - \frac{\beta g}{P\alpha^2 S^*}$$

In other words, the level of effort E_0 of free access equilibrium:

$$E_0 = \frac{g}{\alpha} - \frac{\beta g}{P\alpha^2 S^*}$$

By substituting this value in the function which relates the returns or the level of captures with the effort, we obtain:

$$C_0 = \alpha S^* \left(\frac{g}{\alpha} - \frac{\beta g}{P\alpha^2 S^*}\right)\left[1 - \frac{\alpha}{g}\left(\frac{g}{\alpha} - \frac{\beta g}{P\alpha^2 S^*}\right)\right]$$

It can be noticed now that fishing effort E^* of equilibrium with only one agent is lower than effort E_m, which corresponds to the maximum captures and which is also lower than effort E_0 -captures with free access-.

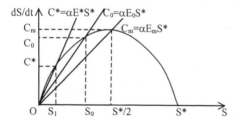

Fig. 5.16

The difference between the efforts is:

$$\Delta E_m = E_m - E^* = \beta g / (2PS^*\alpha^2)$$

On the other hand:

$\Delta E_0 = E_0 - E^* = g \, (PS^*\alpha - 3 \, \beta) / (2PS^*\alpha^2)$

We conclude that, given that the levels of effort are:

$E_m > E_0 > E^*$

The corresponding returns or captures are:

$C_m > C_0 > C^*$

The most efficient solution from the economic point of view is only one agent-owner of all the fish resources as compared with the situation of free access to resources exploitation. Naturally, the idea of only one agent-owner may be replaced with a set of rules which must be obeyed with by different agents, if not many, allowing the joint maximization of profits. A public regulation which establishes the limits for captures in C_0 could also exist.

The use of the fish resources, pastures for cattle, game and tree felling and burning are similar cases. All these are renewable resources which require a rational exploitation under individual agreements or regulation.

Oil and carbon exploitation presents different features since they are non renewable resources.

However, making a detailed analysis of this characteristic, problems are very similar to those dealt with for the fish resources. If too many people extract oil global extractions decrease although the resources extinguish more quickly.

The problems presented above for the natural resources may be extended to other problems in the world. Thus, traffic jams can be analyzed by means of a formal scheme similar to that used for fishing. Transport lines may also generate "congestion of the companies" which compete in the same line, thus leading to congestion in the exploitation of a collectively-owned resource. Moreover, radio frequencies, television waves, internet network, etc, are also subjected to congestion problems and such problems can be dealt with from a formal point of view similarly to the fish resources here exposed.

5.6.1.2.3 Renewable Natural Resources and the Dynamic Analysis: An Application of the Theory of Optimum Control

The above-described bioeconomic model started from the logistics curve which measures the growth of the following fishing biomass:

$$S_t = gS_0 \left[\frac{S_0}{gS^*} + \left(1 - \frac{S_0}{S^*}\right) e^{gt} \right]$$

where S_t provides the level of population or the amount of resource in moment t, S_0 is the corresponding level for the initial period; S^* accounts for the natural equilibrium of population or the maximum amount of population sustainable by the environment in the lack of human commercial activity; g is the intrinsic growth rate to which the vegetative growth rate is approximated when the population tends to zero; and t represents time. The formalized analysis of the bioeconomic model consisted on a static analysis which considered the following initial curve.

$$S = gS \left[\frac{S}{gS^*} + \left(1 - \frac{S_0}{S^*}\right) e^{gt} \right]$$

That is to say:

$$S = gS^2 \frac{1}{gS^*} + gSe^{gt} - g\frac{S^2}{S^*} e^{gt}$$

By deriving with respect to time:

$$\frac{dS}{dt} = g\left(gSe^{gt} - g\frac{S^2}{S^*} e^{gt} \right)$$

$$\frac{1}{g}\frac{dS}{dt} = gSe^{gt}\left(1 - \frac{S^2}{S^*}\right) + \frac{gS^2}{gS^*} - \frac{gS^2}{gS^*}$$

$$\frac{1}{g}\frac{dS}{dt} = S - \frac{S^2}{S^*}$$

$$\frac{dS}{dt} = g\left(S - \frac{S^2}{S^*} \right) = gS\left(1 - \frac{S}{S^*}\right)$$

And after this, the resource income (or level of fishing captures) was presented such as:

$$Y = \alpha E S$$

where E represented the effort and $\alpha > 0$ was a positive parameter.

The model equilibrium enabled us to determine the value of the optimum effort E*, obtaining from this the optimum level of captures. The bioeconomic equilibrium calculated in this way - or point of maximum profit - corresponds to a static equilibrium. In other words, it is assumed that time does not influence the decisions which affect the management of the non renewable resource. However, such an assumption is not very realistic. Consider that the management of any resource is a dynamic process and decisions must be made in a non-temporal context. We will continue with the bioeconomic model in order to illustrate a dynamic decision-making. Thus, the owner of a fishing area will have the objective of determining the level of exploitation of the resource over time C(t) which will provide him with the maximum profit. In other words:

$$\max CNV = \int_0^\infty [P(t) - MC(S)] C(t) e^{-rt} dt$$

s. to $\quad S_0 = 0$

Where the restrictions are state equations and P (t), MC (S) are the price and cost per unit of resources in year t. On the other hand, r is the discount rate and S_0 is the initial level of resources (assumed as known) for the initial year; C(t) is the level of exploitation of the resource (captures) which will be function of the level of S and of applied effort E.

The above optimum control problem gives the solution:

$$F'(S) - C'(S)\,F(S) = r - P'(t)/[P(t) - MC(S)]$$

In order to understand the economic meaning of the above statement, consider that captures in the initial year have a null cost. If this is the case, in the above statement $C'(S) = 0$ and MC $(S) = 0$ it is possible to write:

$$F'(S) + P'(t)/P(t) = r$$

Where F'(S) is the marginal product of resource S and where $P'(t)/P(t)$ is the growth rate of prices.

If $P'(t)/P(t) > 0$ it is not convenient to exploit the fishing renewable resource since F'(S) > r, the marginal productivity of the resource is higher than the discount rate (or marginal cost of non-fishing). The value of the asset renewable resource grows more quickly than the discount rate and its exploitation is not convenient.

If $P'(t)/P(t) < 0$, exploitation of the resource is convenient since the value of the asset resource grows less quickly than the discount rate.

Finally, if $P'(t)/P(t) = 0$ then F'(S) = r obtains the market return and exploitation of the resource is suitable. When interest rates are higher, the resources are intensely exploited and net loss - and even collapse - of the resource will be produced. High interest rates and protection of renewable resources, environment, etc. are incompatible.

On the contrary, a policy of low interest rates may promote the conservation and preservation of renewable natural resources although it must be said that this is also kept for non renewable resources.

5.6.1.2.4 Non Renewable Natural Resources (NRNR)

As already defined, non renewable natural resources are those whose consumption leads to the exhaustion or decrease of the world stock. Examples of these resources are carbon, oil, natural gas, etc. The essential question as regards these resources is: how could they be adequately or optimally exploited?

In order to answer this question we will develop a very simple model.

5.6.1.2.4.1 NRNR Model for the Optimum Extraction

Assumptions

1. The stock $\overline{S}$ of a natural resource is accurately known.
2. Extraction costs are null C = 0; MC= 0.
3. The amount of resource extracted S does not affect price.
4. The price is a known time function, that is to say P = P (t).

A natural resource bed is detected and the question is: when should we start to exploit it? The answer from the economic point of view is: "when the current net value of the investment is the maximum".

Thus, for a discount rate r and a situation of continuous accruing of interests, the CNV is:

$$CNV = \overline{S}\ P(t)\ e^{-rt}$$

and the problem will be now:

$$\max CNV = \overline{S}\ P(t)\ e^{-rt}$$

from where the first order condition is:

$$dCNV\ /\ dt = \overline{S}\ P'(t)\ e^{-rt} - r\overline{S}\ P(t)\ e^{-rt} = 0$$

by dividing the above statement by $\overline{S}\ e^{-rt}$ we obtain:

$$P'(t) - r\ P(t) = 0$$

which is the equilibrium condition $P'(t)\ /\ P(t) = r$. The second order condition is:

$$d^2CNV\ /\ dt^2 = P''(t) - r\ P'(t) < 0$$

in other words

$$P''(t)\ /\ P'(t) = r$$

Then, the CNV will be maximum when the rate of price variation equals the discount or interest rate r. Moreover, by the second order condition we know that if $P'(t)\ /\ P(t) > r$ the non renewable resource must not be exploited. In addition, if $P'(t)\ /\ P(t) < r$ it is convenient to exploit the non renewable resource. Let's see why. If $P'(t)\ /\ P(t) > r$ the marginal value of non extraction exceeds the marginal cost of non extraction and therefore, exploitation of the resource is not convenient. However, if $P'(t)\ /\ P(t) < r$ extracting the resource is interesting because the marginal value of non extracting is lower than the marginal cost of non extracting.

On the other hand, if an employer owns a bed and does not exploit the non renewable resource, after some time, it will have an accumulated wealth of

$$\overline{S}\ P(t) + \overline{S}\ P'(t)$$

Nonetheless, if the resource is exploited, we will have that:

$$\overline{S}\ P(t) + r\ \overline{S}\ P'(t) = (1+r)\ \overline{S}\ P(t)$$

If we equal now the two final wealth stocks

$$\overline{S}\ P(t) + r\ \overline{S}\ P'(t) = (1+r)\ \overline{S}\ P(t)$$

then

$$P'(t) = r\ P(t)$$

from where

$$P'(t)\ /\ P(t) = r$$

first order condition of equilibrium.

If we introduce now the modification $C \neq 0$ and therefore $MC \neq 0$ we can write that:

$$CNV = \overline{S} \ P(t) \ e^{-rt} - MC \ \overline{S} \ e^{-rt}$$

Then we must maximize

$$\max CNV = [\overline{S} \ P(t) - MC \ \overline{S}] e^{-rt}$$

The first order condition is

$$dCNV / dt = P'(t) - r \ P(t) + r \ MC = 0$$

Then

$$P'(t) / [P(t) - MC] = r$$

Where $[P(t) - MC]$ can be denominated user's cost or cost for future generations. The second order condition is:

$$P''(t) / [P'(t) - MC'] < r$$

This new equilibrium condition states that the marginal value of non extracting $[P'(t)]$ equals the Marginal Cost of non extracting $[P(t) - r \ MC]$, therefore, extracting is convenient when the marginal value of non extracting is lower than the marginal cost of non extracting, that is to say, when $P'(t) < r \ P(t) - r \ MC$. Otherwise, the resource must not be extracted.

Optimum Extraction and Price Paths
The above model can be modified in its third assumption now assuming that there is an inverse relationship between price and the extracted amount. In line with this, S_t, the amount of resource extracted in moment t, has an inverse relationship with

$$P_t = P(S_t), P'(S_t) > 0$$

Again, the maximum problem is:

$$\max CNV = \overline{S} \ P(S_t) \ e^{-rt}$$

and the first order condition is

$$d \ CNV / dt = \overline{S} \ P'(S_t) \ e^{-rt} - r \ \overline{S} \ P(S_t) \ e^{-rt} = 0$$

from where

$$P'(S_t) - r \ P(S_t) = 0$$

or

$$d \ P(S_t) / dt - r \ P(S_t) = 0$$

from where

$$d \ P(S_t) - r \ P(S_t) \ dt = 0$$

$$d \ P(S_t) = r \ P(S_t) \ dt$$

by integrating

$\int dP(S_t) / P(S_t) = \int r\, dt$

$Ln\, P(S_t) + C_0 = rt + C_1$

from where

$P(S_t) = e^{rt} \cdot e^{C_1 - C_0} = 1/k \cdot e^{rt}$

if we make $t = 0$, then

$P_0 = 1/k$

so a specific solution of the differential equation is:

$P_t = P_0\, e^{rt}$

where P_0 is the price of the resource the first day of extracting.

Now let T the extracting horizon or the period during which we will extract from the resource until its stock $\overline{S}$ runs out, then, it will be verified that:

$\int_0^T S_t\, dt = \overline{S}$

Therefore, considering an inverse linear demand such as

$P_t = \alpha - \beta\, S_t, \text{con } \beta > 0$

and substituting:

$\int_0^T (\alpha - P_t)/\beta\, dt = \overline{S}$

by substituting $P_t = P_0\, e^{rt}$ we obtain

$$\int_0^T \frac{\alpha - P_0 e^{rt}}{\beta} dt = \frac{\alpha T}{\beta} - \frac{P_0}{r\beta}(1 + e^{rt}) = \overline{S}$$

On the other hand, given that the demand equation is dependent negative with respect to price and inverse with respect to the amount, the higher amount of resource is exploited, the higher the price will be. This is represented in the following system:

$P_0\, e^{rt} = \alpha$

$$\frac{\alpha T}{\beta} - \frac{P_0}{r\beta}(1 + e^{rt}) = \overline{S}$$

In which it is possible to obtain P_0 as well as the optimum extracting horizon or optimum exploitation of resource T and, such values being known, it is possible to obtain the optimum extraction and price paths.

5.6.1.2.4.2 NRNR Model with Interests for Future Generations (Exogenous Treatment)

The cost for future generations derived from the using up of a resource by present or former generations must be included in some way in the non renewable resource models.

On the whole, a non renewable resource is a production input and it is widely known that an input demand is obtained from its marginal product value (MPV). Moreover, this input also has a MC of resource extraction. An equilibrium for the present generation can be represented as in figure 5.1:

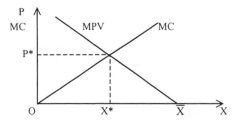

Fig. 5.17

where (X*, P*) are the optimum quantity and price of extraction or of the input.

We consider the interests for future generations to be a cost for them due to the fact that the resource is not available for them or that it is available in lower amounts. Such a cost will be denominated MCFG and now it is possible to represent:

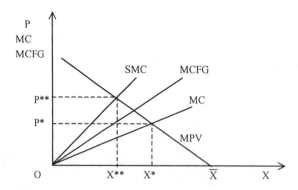

Fig. 5.18

where SMC is the social marginal cost which results from the addition of the cost of the extracted unit for the present generation and the cost for future generations. This means that the amount and the price of equilibrium are (X**, P**).

The significant intergenerational efficiency requires higher prices and smaller extraction quantities.

Practical Case

Let us consider a resource bed where demand is:

$P_t = 10 - X_t$

and the extracting cost is:

$MC = 0.5X$

with a marginal cost for future generations with the following value:

$MCFG = X - 1$

in other words, the first unit extracted does not represent any cost for future generations.

Estimate the optimum level of extracting considering the interests for the present generation and those for future generations.

The equilibrium for the present generation is:

$MC = MPV$

$0.5X_t = 10 - X_t; \ 0.5X_t + X_t = 10$

from where

$1.5 \ X_t = 10; \ X_t^* = 10/1.5 = 6.66$

and therefore:

$P_t^* = 10 - 6.66 = 3.33.$

Considering now the interests for future generations, in this case we will have:

$MCFG = X - 1$

then,

$SMC = MC + MCFG = 0.5 \ X_t + X_t - 1$

therefore

$0.5 \ X_t + X_t - 1 = 10 - X_t$

then

$10 - X_t - 0.5 \ X_t - X_t + 1 = 0; \ 2.5 \ X_t = 11; \ X_t^* = 11/2.5 = 4.4$

and by substituting in the demand

$P_t^* = 10 - 4.4 = 5.6 \text{m.u.}$

This means that the present generation, without taking into account the interests for the future generation, consumes an allocative surplus of inefficiency of 2.27 physical units.

The consumer's surplus for the situation where the interests for future generations are ignored, is equal to:

$\int_0^{6,67} (10 - X)\, dX - 6.67\,(3.3) = 22.22$ m.u.

If the present consumer takes into account future generations his surplus will be:

$\int_0^{4,40} (10 - X)\, dX = 4.40\,(5.60) = 9.68$ m.u.

In other words, for the present consumer, taking into account the interests of future generations implies a loss of 12.54 m.u.

Practical Case
A resource bed stock - for instance, carbon - is estimated at 10 units. The inverse demand for carbon is:

$P_t = 10\text{-}X_t$

and the interest or discount rate is 2%.

We want to determine the optimum extraction path and the optimum price path.

In order to solve this problem, we use the traditional approach which maximizes the current net value (CNV) or the resource, in other words:

$\max_t \text{CNV} = \overline{X}\, P_t\, e^{-rt}$

from where,

$d\text{CNV} / dt = \overline{X}\, P_t{'}\, e^{-rt} - r\, \overline{X}\, P_t\, e^{-rt} = 0$

and by dividing it all by $\overline{X}\, e^{-rt}$ we can write:

$P_t{'} - r\, P_t = 0$

that is to say:

$P_t{'} / P_t = r$

On the other hand,

$d^2\, \text{CNV} / dt^2 = P_t{''} - r\, P_t{'} < 0$

from where,

$P_t{''} / P_t{'} < r$

From the first order condition it is possible to write:

$dP_t / dt = r\, P_t$

by separating variables

$dP_t / P_t = r\, dt$

by integrating

$\int dP_t / P_t = r \int dt$

and now solving

$\text{Ln}\,(P_t \cdot k) = rt,\ \text{o bien, Ln}\, P_t + \text{Ln}\, k = rt$

where k is a constant:

$P_t\, k = e^{rt}$

from where

$P_t = 1/k \cdot e^{rt}$

In order to eliminate the integration constant $1/k$ we make $t = 0$, thus obtaining:

$P_0 = 1/k \cdot e^0 = 1/k$

so the specific solution of the differential equation under the Hotelling Rule is:

$P_t = P_0 e^{rt}$

On the other hand, given that the temporal horizon of carbon extracting is t and the stock is $\overline{X}$, it will be verified that:

$\int_0^t X_t dt = \overline{X}$

Now, with the following equations

$P_t = P_0 e^{rt}$ (5.1)

$\int_0^t X_t dt = \overline{X}$ (5.2)

we can obtain the initial price and the optimum mining of the resource carbon as the demand function of carbon is:

$P_t = 10 - X_t; \; 10 - P_t = X_t$

by substituting in (5.2)

$\int_0^t (10 - P_t) \, dt = \overline{X}$

and now by substituting (5.1) in the above statement

$\int_0^t (10 - P_0 e^{rt}) \, dt = \overline{X}$

$10 \int_0^t dt - \int_0^t P_0 e^{rt} dt = 10t - P_0 (1 + e^{rt}) = \overline{X}$

$-\int_0^t P_0 e^{rt} dt = -P_0 e^{r0} - P_0 e^{rt} = -P_0 - P_0 e^{rt} = -P_0 (1 + e^{rt}) = \overline{X}$

The system to be now solved is:

$P_0 e^{0.02t} = 10$

$10 t + 50 P_0 (1 - P_0 e^{0.02t}) = 10$

The solution to the non-linear system is $t = 10.34$ and $P_0 = 8.13$.

The optimum extraction and price paths can be exposed as follows:

$P_0 e^{0.02T} = 10$

$S_t = 10 - P_t$

where S_t is the optimum quantity to extract, P_t is the optimum extracting price and t is the optimum use of the resource.

For a solution $P_0 = 8.13$, $t = 10.34$ we have table 5.1.

Table 5.1

YEAR (t)	PRICE (P_t)	QUANTITY/IES	STOCK (S* - S)
0	8.13	1.87	8.13
1	8.29	1.71	6.42
2	8.46	1.54	4.88
3	8.63	1.37	3.51
4	8.80	1.20	2.31
5	8.99	1.01	1.30
6	9.17	0.83	0.47
7	9.35	0.65	-0.18
8	9.54	0.46	-0.64
9	9.73	0.27	-0.91
10	9.93	0.07	-0.98
10.34*	10	0	-0.98

In this case, unless more reserves than those estimated are found, the resource will be exhaustred in the sixth year of extracting.

Imagine now the following situation:

$P_0 = 2.74$; t = 64

Table 5.2

YEAR (t)	PRICE (P_t)	QUANTITY/IES	STOCK (S* -S)
0	2.74	7.26	2.74
1	2.80	7.20	-4.46
2	2.85	7.15	-11.61
...	...	...	...
...	...	...	...
64	9.85	0.15	-...
64.7*	10	0	-...

In table 5.2, unless more reserves than those estimated are found the resource will be extinguished in the first year of extracting.

In both tables we can observe that as stock decreases the quantity extracted becomes lower.

5.6.1.2.4.3 NRNR Model with Interests for Future Generations (Endogenous Treatment)

The exogenous treatment model determined "ad hoc" the cost for future generations of the non-availability of resources or simply of having less resources available. It is very difficult to deal with this matter as we do not know is the cost for future generations of the non-availability of a resource. This question will be dealt with through the maximization of the current non-temporal net value (CNV) (assuming that the quantity extracted does not affect price) of the following type:

$$\max \text{CNV} = (P_0 X_0 - CX_0) + (P_1 X_1 - CX_1)(1+r)^{-1} + ... + (P_t X_t - CX_t)(1+r)^{-t^*}$$

s. to: $X_0 + X_1 + ... + X_{t^*} = \overline{X}$

where (P_0, X_0) are the price and the initial quantity respectively; C is extracting cost per unit or marginal cost always considered as constant; r is the discount or interest rate; t* is the extracting horizon and finally, $\overline{X}$ is the non renewable resource stock.

The intermediate Lagrange function will be:

$$L = \Sigma_{t=0}^{t^*}(P_t X_t - CX_t)(1+r)^{-t} + \lambda(\overline{X} - \Sigma_{t=0}^{t^*} X_t)$$

where λ is the Lagrange multiplier, t represents each moment of time and t* is the extracting horizon. λ represents the quantity which the CNV increases if the stock increases in one unit, in other words, λ is the shadow price of the current resource so it can represent a good approximation to the cost for future generations.

The first order conditions are:

$$\frac{\partial L}{\partial X_0} = P_0 - C - \lambda = 0$$

$$\frac{\partial L}{\partial X_1} = (P_1 - C) \cdot (1+r)^{-1} - \lambda = 0$$

....

$$\frac{\partial L}{\partial X_{t^*}} = (P_{t^*} - C) \cdot (1+r)^{-t^*} - \lambda = 0$$

From the first derivative we obtain:

$$P_0 - C = \lambda$$

that is to say, the shadow price of the resource is equal to the price of the resource in initial period P_0 less extracting cost C.

On the other hand, the current value of the shadow price or cost for future generations will be:

$$P_0 - C = \frac{P_1 - C}{(1+r)} = \frac{P_2 - C}{(1+r)^2} = ... = \frac{P_{t^*} - C}{(1+r)^{t^*}} = \lambda$$

in other words, the current value of the cost for future generations is always constant and its value is λ.

In general terms:

$$P_t = C + \lambda (1+r)^t = C + (P_0 - C)(1+r)^t$$

This equation provides the optimum price path

Let's assume now that the quantity extracted actually affects price and also that the MC of the extraction depends on the extracted volume. In this case:

$$\max \pi = \int_0^{X_0} (a - 2bx - c) \, dx + \int_0^{X_1} (a - 2bx - c) (1+r)^{-1} \, dx + ...+$$

$$+\int_0^{X_{t^*}} (a - 2bx - c) (1+r)^{-t^*} \, dx$$

s. to: $X_0 + X_1 + ... + X_{t^*} = \overline{X}$

and the first order conditions are:

$$\frac{\partial L}{\partial X_0} = a - 2bX_0 - C - \lambda = 0$$

$$\frac{\partial L}{\partial X_1} = (a - 2bX_1 - C) \cdot (1+r)^{-1} - \lambda = 0$$

....

$$\frac{\partial L}{\partial X_{t^*}} = (a - 2bX_{t^*} - C) \cdot (1+r)^{-t^*} - \lambda = 0$$

from where

$$\lambda = a - 2bX_0 - C$$

where we obtain λ, X_0, $X_1, ... X_{t^*}$ and, by substituting these quantities in the demand function we have:

$$P_t = a - b X_t$$

thus obtaining the optimum price path.

Practical Case

Assuming a resource with an extracting horizon $t^* = 3$ years; a discount rate $r = 10\%$; a demand function $P_t = 10 - X_t$ and marginal costs $C = 0,5X$.

Estimate the intergenerational net social profit maximization.

$$\max \pi = \int_0^{X_0} (10 - X - 0,5X) \, dx + \int_0^{X_1} (10 - X - 0,5X) (1+r)^{-1} \, dx +$$

$+ \int_0^{X_2} (10\text{-}X\text{-}0,5X)(1+r)^{-2} dx$

s. to: $X_0 + X_1 + X_2 = 10$

The first order conditions are:

$$\frac{\partial L}{\partial X_0} = 10 - 1,5X_0 - \lambda = 0$$

$$\frac{\partial L}{\partial X_1} = 9,09 - 1,36X_1 - \lambda = 0$$

$$\frac{\partial L}{\partial X_2} = 8,26 - 1,24X_2 - \lambda = 0$$

$X_0 + X_1 + X_2 = 10$

By solving the system we obtain:

$\lambda = 4,53$

$X_0 = 3,64$

$X_1 = 3,35$

$X_2 = 3,01$

and by substituting in the demand equation we have:

$P_t = 10 - X_t$

thus obtaining the optimum price path.

$P_0 = 6,36$

$P_1 = 6,65$

$P_2 = 6,69$

5.6.1.3 Common Property Resources

There are goods that are of common property by tradition or custom. This is the case of municipal pasturelands. The optimization problem can be exposed as follows. Be $x_i = x(y)$ the production function of stock farmer i, where x_i represents the quantity of output produced (for instance, milk) and where y represents the number of cows. This production function satisfies that:

$$\frac{\partial x(y)}{\partial y} > 0; \quad \frac{\partial^2 x(y)}{\partial y^2} < 0.$$

Stock farmer i will try to solve the following problem:

max $p - zy$

s. to: $x_i = x(y)$

Where p is the price of output x and z is the price of input y.
The first order condition is:

$$\frac{\partial px(y)}{\partial y} - z = 0$$

With the unit price p we obtain:

$$\frac{\partial x(y)}{\partial y} = z$$

In other words:

$$MPg_y = z$$

However, since there are i stock farmers and each one can send cows to the common pastureland, being a finite resource, when a stock farmer takes into account the possibility of adding one more cow, he compares $x(y)$ – income – with z – cost -. If the total of cows is ω we can see that stock farmers will take more cows to the pastureland until profits are zero, that is to say:

$$x(\omega) - z\,\omega = 0$$

from where

$$x(\omega) / \omega = z$$

where the mean product MeP_y equals z.

The problem is that each one can increase the number of cows as he wishes since he does not consider the "social cost" or the cost for the others derived from taking his cows to the pasturelands.
Graphically:

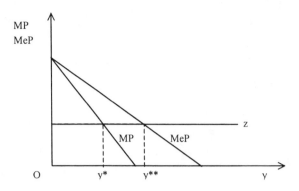

Fig. 5.19

Where y* is the level of efficient production and y** is the level of equilibrium production for stock farmers. An overexploitation of the pasturelands takes place with a surplus quantity of cows y** - y*. The only way to correct this situation is to establish a regulation of y* number of cows which can pasture at the municipal pasturelands.

5.6.1.4 Externalities

5.6.1.4.1 Externalities in the Production of Partial Equilibrium

In order to explain the concept of externalities we will use the case of two firms. Firm 1 produces a quantity x_1 of steel and a specific quantity x_2 of wastage flowing into a river. Firm 2 produces quantity x_3 of fresh fish and it is located down the river, so it is damaged by the wastage of firm x_1.

The cost function of firm 1 is $C_1 = C_1(x_1, x_2)$ while the cost function of firm 2 is $C_2 = C_2(x_3, x_2)$ where:

$$\partial C_2 / \partial x_2 > 0$$

in other words, wastage has increased the cost of fish production, and where:

$$\partial C_1 / \partial x_2 \leq 0$$

in other words, wastage reduces the cost of steel production.

The steel mill, firm 1, tries to maximize:

$$\max_{x_1, x_2} P_1 x_1 - C_1(x_1, x_2)$$

Instead the fish farm, firm 2, tries to maximize:

$$\max_{x_3} P_3 x_3 - C_2(x_3, x_2)$$

The first order conditions for firm 1 are:

$$\frac{\partial \pi_1}{\partial x_1} = P_1 - \frac{\partial C_1(x_1, x_2)}{\partial x_1} = 0 \Rightarrow P_1 = \frac{\partial C_1(x_1, x_2)}{\partial x_1}$$

$$\frac{\partial \pi_1}{\partial x_2} = 0 - \frac{\partial C_2(x_3, x_2)}{\partial x_2} = 0 \Rightarrow 0 = \frac{\partial C_2(x_3, x_2)}{\partial x_2}$$

The first order conditions for firm 2 are:

$$\frac{\partial \pi_1}{\partial x_3} = P_3 - \frac{\partial C_2(x_3, x_2)}{\partial x_3} = 0 \Rightarrow P_3 = \frac{\partial C_3(x_3, x_2)}{\partial x_3}$$

that is to say:

$$P_1 = MC_{x_1}$$

$$P_3 = MCg_{x_3}$$

$$P_2 = MC_{x_2} = 0$$

In other words, the price of the increase in production of each good – steel and fish – must equal the MC. In the case of the steel mill the price of wastage is null, therefore, wastage will be produced until $MC_{x_2} = 0$ and it will stop being produced when the cost of an additional wastage unit is positive ($MC_{x_2} > 0$).

It is expected that too much wastage is produced from the social point of view.
Solutions:

i) Merging the steel mill with the fish farm.
ii) Fixing taxes.
iii) Creating a market of rights of wastage production.

5.6.1.4.1.1 External Cost Internalization: Merging of Firms

i) *Merging of firm 1 with 2:*

$$\max \pi_c = P_1 x_1 + P_3 x_3 - C_1(x_1, x_2) - C_2(x_3, x_2)$$

$$x_1, x_2, x_3$$

the first order conditions are:

$$\frac{\partial \pi_c}{\partial x_1} = P_1 - \frac{\partial C_1}{\partial x_1} = 0$$

$$\frac{\partial \pi_c}{\partial x_3} = P_3 - \frac{\partial C_2}{\partial x_3} = 0$$

$$\frac{\partial \pi_c}{\partial x_2} = \frac{\partial C_1}{\partial x_2} + \frac{\partial C_2}{\partial x_2}$$

So, when the steel mill decides what quantity of wastage must be produced, it will consider the effects of its decision on the profits of the fish farm.

The merger produces wastage until $MC^1x_2 + MC^2x_2 = 0$.

In other words:

$$-MC^1x_2 = MC^2x_2$$

where the MCx_2 is positive since the higher wastage is the higher the cost of producing a given quantity of fish will be. Therefore, the merger wishes to produce where it is verified that the $(-MCx_2)$ is positive.

Graphically:

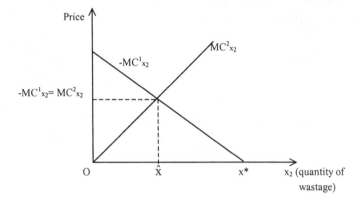

Fig. 5.20

Where $\hat{x}$ is the optimum quantity from the social point of view and x^* is the optimum quantity from the individual point of view.

5.6.1.4.1.2 Pigouvian or Optimum Taxes

ii) Pigouvian taxes and efficiency
Assume that the government fixes a tax t per each wastage unit produced by the steel mill -firm 1- therefore:

$$\max_{x_1, x_2} \pi_1 = P_1x_1 - C_1(x_1, x_2) - t x_2$$

The first order conditions are:

$$\frac{\partial \pi_1}{\partial x_1} = P_1 - \frac{\partial C_1}{\partial x_1} = 0 \Rightarrow P_1 = \frac{\partial C_1}{\partial x_1}$$

$$\frac{\partial \pi_2}{\partial x_2} = -\frac{\partial C_1}{\partial x_2} - t = 0 \Rightarrow t = -\frac{\partial C_1}{\partial x_2}$$

t is a Pigouvian tax [A.C. Pigou (1877-1959)] but we need to know the optimum wastage in order to fix that tax. However, if we knew this optimum wastage we could also tell the steel mill to produce the exact quantity of it and it would not be necessary to introduce the tax.

5.6.1.4.1.3 Externalities Market

iii) Creation of markets of rights of wastage production.
Assume that the fish farm has the right to have pure water but it can sell this right. Therefore, being P_2 the price per wastage unit and x_2 the quantity of wastage, the problem for the fish farm would now be:

$$\max_{x_3, x_2} = P_3 x_3 + P_2 x_2 - C_2 (x_3, x_2) = \pi_2$$

and for the steel mill would be:

$$\max_{x_1, x_2} = P_1 x_1 - P_2 x_2 - C_1 (x_1, x_2) = \pi_1$$

Term $P_2 x_2$ has a negative sign for the steel mill and a positive sign for the fish farm since the steel mill must buy the right to produce wastage from the fish farm. The maximization conditions of π_2 and π_1 are:

$P_1 = MC_{x_1}; P_1 = \partial C_1 / \partial x_1$

$P_2 = MC^1_{x_2}; P_2 = - \partial C_1 / \partial x_2$

$P_2 = MC^2_{x_2}; P_2 = \partial C_2 / \partial x_2$

$P_3 = MC_{x_3}; P_3 = \partial C_2 / \partial x_3$

therefore, each firm faces the social marginal cost of each one of its actions.
Observe that:

$-MC^1_{x_2} = MC^2_{x_2}$

or that:

$MC^1_{x_2} + MC^2_{x_2} = 0$

In other words, the marginal cost incurred by the steel mill for reducing wastage must equal the marginal profit obtained by the fish farm as a consequence of such a reduction.

We have said that the fish farm had the right to have pure water and that the steel mill had the right to produce wastage, however, if we had assigned the property rights the other way round the steel mill would have the right to produce wastage and the fish farm would have to pay for the steel mill to reduce wastage.

The only change is the distribution of profits between the firms. This is widely known as the Coase Theorem.

5.6.1.4.1.3.1 The Coase Theorem

Under some specific circumstances, if there are not "effects – income", the efficient quantity of the good which implies externalities is independent from the distribution of property rights. In the different Pereto efficient allocations, consumers have various quantities of money but the quantity of the externality is independent from wealth distribution.

5.6.1.4.2 Externalities in a EG Model, 2 Producers, 2 Consumers and 2 Goods

An economy with 2 individuals – 1 and 2 – producing and consuming two goods x_1 and x_2 from the following production functions:

$$x_1 = f_1 (y_1)$$

$$x_2 = f_2 (y_2, x_1)$$

In other words, the production of the first firm produces an external effect on the second one, which will be positive or negative depending on the sign of $\partial f_2 / \partial x_1$.

The quantity available of the productive input is $\bar{y} = y_1 + y_2$, w is its price and P_1, P_2 are the prices of x_1 and x_2.

For firm 1 the problem is:

$$\left. \begin{array}{l} \max \pi_1 = x_1 P_1 - w\, y_1 \\[2mm] \text{s. to: } x_1 = f_1(y_1) \end{array} \right\} \max \pi_1 = f_1(y_1)P_1 - w\, y_1$$

whose first order condition is:

$$\frac{d\pi_1}{dy_1} = \frac{\partial f_1}{\partial y_1} P_1 - w = 0 \; ; \quad \frac{df_1}{dP_1} = \frac{w}{P_1} \; .$$

For firm 2:

$$\left. \begin{array}{l} \max \pi_2 = x_2 P_2 - w\, y_2 \\[2mm] \text{s. to: } x_2 = f_2(y_2, x_1) \end{array} \right\} \max \pi_2 = f_2(y_2, x_1) - w\, y_2$$

whose first order conditions are:

$$\frac{d\pi_2}{dy_2} = \frac{\partial f_2(y_2, x_1)}{\partial y_2} P_2 - w = 0$$

$$\frac{d\pi_2}{dx_1} = \frac{\partial f_2(y_2, x_1)}{\partial x_1} P_2 = 0$$

that is to say:

$$\frac{\partial f_2(y_2, x_1)}{\partial y_2} = \frac{w}{P_2} \Rightarrow \frac{\partial f_2(y_2, x_1)}{\partial y_2} P_2 = w$$

from where:

$$\frac{df_1}{dy_1} = \frac{w}{P_1} \Rightarrow \frac{df_1}{dy_1} P_1 = w$$

therefore:

$$\frac{\partial f_2}{\partial y_2} P_2 = \frac{df_1}{dy_1} P_1$$

in other words, the equilibrium condition (EGC) for the two firms is:

$$\frac{\partial f_2 / \partial y_2}{df_1 / dy_1} = \frac{P_1}{P_2}$$

on the other hand:

$$x_1 = f_1(y_1)$$

and differentiating with respect to y_1

$$\frac{dx_1}{dy_1} = \frac{df_1(y_1)}{dy_1} \Rightarrow dx_1 = \frac{df_1}{dy_1} dy_1$$

$$x_2 = f_2(y_2, x_1)$$

partially differentiating:

$$dx_2 = \frac{\partial f_2}{\partial y_2} dy_2 + \frac{\partial f_2}{\partial x_1} dx_1$$

and given that $\bar{y} = y_1 + y_2$, by differentiating:

$$d\bar{y} = 0 = dy_1 + dy_2$$

in other words:

$$dy_1 + dy_2 = 0$$

by substituting:

$$dx_2 = \frac{\partial f_2}{\partial y_2} dy_2 + \frac{\partial f_2}{\partial x_1} \left(\frac{df_1}{dy_1} \right) dy_1$$

$$dx_2 = \frac{\partial f_2}{\partial y_2}(-dy_1) + \frac{\partial f_2}{\partial x_1}dx_1$$

$$dx_2 = -\frac{\partial f_2 / \partial y_2}{df_1 / dy_1}dx_1 + \frac{\partial f_2}{\partial x_1}dx_1$$

from where:

$$dx_2 = \left(-\frac{\partial f_2 / \partial y_2}{df_1 / dy_1} + \frac{\partial f_2}{\partial x_1}\right)dx_1$$

thus:

$$-\frac{dx_2}{dx_1} = \frac{\partial f_2 / \partial y_2}{df_1 / dy_1} - \frac{\partial f_2}{\partial x_1}$$

where $-dx_2/dx_1$ = Marginal Rate of Transformation.

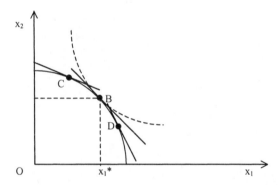

Fig. 5.21

the external effect will be null if $\partial f_2 / \partial x_1 = 0$ and the and the equilibrium will be point B (x^*_1, x^*_2).
However, if $\partial f_2 / \partial x_1 < 0$, then (-)· (-) = (+). We will have the equilibrium point D, in other words, an excessive quantity of the good is produced, which generates negative external effect (x'_1). On the other hand, if $\partial f_2 / \partial x_1 > 0$ then (-)· (+) = (-) and we will have equilibrium point C, that is to say, an insufficient quantity of the good is produced, which generates a positive external effect (x''_1).

Assume now that we make explicit the existence of each consumer whose utility functions are:

$$U_1 = U_1(x_1, x_2)$$

$U_2=U_2(x_1, x_2)$

The problem for individual 1 is now:

max $U_1= U_1(x_1, x_2)$

s. to: $x_1 = f_1(y_1)$

$x_2 = f_2(y_2, x_1)$

$\overline{y} = y_1 + y_2$

$x_1, x_2, y_1, y_2 \geq 0$

where,

$L = U_1(x_1, x_2) + \lambda_1 (x_1 - f_1(y_1)) + \lambda_2 (x_2 - f_2(y_2, x_1)) + \mu (\overline{y} - y_1 - y_2)$

the first order conditions are now:

$$\frac{\partial L}{\partial x_1} = \frac{\partial U}{\partial x_1} + \lambda_1 - \lambda_2 \frac{\partial f_2}{\partial x_1} = 0$$

$$\frac{\partial L}{\partial x_2} = \frac{\partial U}{\partial x_2} + \lambda_2 = 0$$

$$\frac{\partial L}{\partial y_1} = -\lambda_1 \frac{df_1(y_1)}{dy_1} - \mu = 0$$

$$\frac{\partial L}{\partial y_2} = -\lambda_2 \frac{\partial f_2}{\partial y_2} - \mu = 0$$

and as regards consumption we have:

$$\frac{\partial U / \partial x_1}{dU / dx_2} = \frac{-\lambda_1 + \lambda_2 \, \partial f_2 / \partial x_1}{-\lambda_2} = \frac{\lambda_1}{\lambda_2} - \frac{\partial f_2}{\partial x_1}$$

The effect will be again null if $-\partial f_2 / \partial x_1 = 0$, otherwise we will have positive or negative externality.

As regards production:

$$-\lambda_1 \frac{df_1(y_1)}{dy_1} = \mu \; ; -\lambda_2 \frac{\partial f_2}{\partial y_2} = \mu \,;\, \lambda_1 \frac{df_1(y_1)}{dy_1} = \lambda_2 \frac{\partial f_2}{\partial y_2}$$

in other words, the equilibrium conditions (EG) for the 2 firms are:

$$\frac{\lambda_1}{\lambda_2} = \frac{\partial f_2 / \partial y_2}{df_1(y_1) / dy_1}$$

The same happens for individual 2.

The conclusion is clear: if we expose the existence of external effects as a production problem, the general equilibrium condition

$$\text{MRTransformation} = \frac{\partial f_2 / \partial y_2}{df_1 / dy_1} + \frac{\partial f_2}{\partial x_1}$$

leads to an undesirable allocation from the social point of view, too much of the product with negative externalities is produced while little of the product with positive externalities is produced.

If we pose the problem of existence of external effects as a consumption problem, the general equilibrium condition will be:

$$\text{MRSubstitution} = \frac{\partial U / \partial x_1}{\partial U / \partial x_2} + \frac{\partial f_2}{\partial x_1}$$

which leads again to an undesirable allocation from the social point of view, too much of the good with negative externalities is consumed and little of the good with positive externalities is consumed.

This is due to the fact that the external effects are not internalized because there is not a market for them and they lead to non-desirable allocations from the point of view of collective welfare since they do not have an associated price.

In order to solve this problem we have (as in the previous section) three possible solutions:

i) creating markets for the external effect;
ii) merging of firms with external effects;
iii) levying taxes.

The first choice:

i) creating markets for the external effects;

Assume there is a market of rights to wastage production where the government, in the name of those citizens who suffer the external effect, for example, wastage, sells rights to produce wastage at price P_e., therefore, the profit functions of our economy are now:

$$\pi_1(y_1) = P_1 \, f_1(y_1) - w \, y_1 - P_e \, f_1(y_1)$$

$$\pi_2(y_2, x_1) = P_2 \, f_2(y_1, x_1) - w \, y_2 + P_e \, f_1(y_1)$$

Firm 1 acquires the new input "right to produce wastage" and pays P_e to firm 2, which sells rights to produce wastage and therefore, obtains the subsequent returns.

Profit maximization of firm 1 is:

$$\max \pi_1(y_1) = P_1 \, f_1(y_1) - w \, y_1 - P_e \, f_1(y_1)$$

and the first order conditions are:

$d\pi_1/dy_1 = P_1\, df_1/dy_1 - w - P_e\, df_1/dy_1 = 0; (P_1 - P_e)\, df_1/dy_1 = w;$

Profit maximization of firm 2 is:

$\max \pi_2(y_2) = P_2\, f_2(y_2, x_1) - w\, y_2 + P_e\, f_1(y_1)$

and the first order conditions are:

$$\frac{\partial \pi_2}{\partial y_2} = P_2\, \frac{\partial f_2}{\partial y_2} - w = 0 \; ; \; P_2\, \frac{\partial f_2}{\partial y_2} = w \; ;$$

$$\frac{\partial \pi_2}{\partial x_1} = P_2\, \frac{\partial f_2}{\partial x_1} + P_e = 0 \; ; \; P_2\, \frac{\partial f_2}{\partial x_1} = -P_e \; ;$$

By substituting we obtain:

$$\frac{P_1}{w} = \frac{1}{df_1/dy_1} - \frac{\partial f_2/\partial x_1}{\partial f_2/\partial y_2}$$

which provides an efficient solution if:

$$\frac{\partial f_2}{\partial x_1} = 0 \Rightarrow \frac{\partial f_1}{\partial y_1} = \frac{w}{P_1}$$

However, there are at least two problems with difficult solution:

i) the organization of markets of external effects may be very expensive (compare welfare returns with the costs derived from the organization of the market of rights for the external effects);

ii) the non-convexity of the productive technology of external effects avoids the equivalence between GE and PO.

(The problem can be exposed again by changing the signs of P_e. in π_1 and π_2, in other words, by modifying who pays and who receives and the result would not affect the equilibrium conditions but only alter the income distribution of the agents).

The second choice:

ii) Merging of firms: internalization of the effect.

The 2 firms decide to merge in order to maximize in competitive conditions the joint profit:

$\pi_c = P_1\, f_1(y_1) + P_2\, f_2,\, f_1(y_1)) - w\, (y_1 + y_2)$

whose maximum first order conditions are:

$$\frac{\partial \pi_c}{\partial y_1} = P_1 \frac{df_1}{dy_1} + P_2 \frac{\partial f_2}{\partial x_1} \frac{df_1}{dy_1} - w = 0 ;$$

$$\frac{\partial \pi_c}{\partial y_2} = P_2 \frac{\partial f_2}{\partial y_2} - w = 0 ;$$

from which:

$$P_1 \frac{df_1}{dy_1} = w - w \frac{\partial f_2}{\partial x_1} \frac{df_1 / dy_1}{\partial f_2 / \partial y_2} = w\left(1 - \frac{\partial f_2 / \partial x_1}{\partial f_2 / \partial y_2} \frac{df_1}{dy_1}\right) ;$$

which is another Pareto Optimum condition under external effects (and is an efficient solution as in the previous case).

In other words, when both firms merge, the effect produced by the former on the latter is internalized in the sense that it is taken into account when maximizing the joint profit of both firms. Therefore, this effect loses its disruptive character.

The third choice:

iii) Levying taxes: by taxing the external effect.

In order to ensure that the agents act not only taking into account real costs but also considering private costs, the agent which causes the negative external effect can be burdened with a tax. However, this tax must exactly reflect the assessment of the external effect.

Being t the unit tax rate on product x_1, which is paid by the agent causing the effect and transferred to the receiver of such an effect, and which tries to lead to an efficient allocation, the producers profit functions is now:

$$\pi_1(y_1) = (1-t)P_1 f_1(y_1) - w y_1$$

$$\pi_2 = P_2 f_2(y_2, x_1) - w y_2 + t P_1 f_1(y_1)$$

(observe that this is similar to case (i) $P_e = t P_1$).
   For firm 1 the maximum problems are:

$$\max \pi_1 = (1-t) P_1 f_1(y_1) - w y_1$$

$$d\pi_1/dy_1 = (1-t) P_1 df_1(y_1)/dy_1 - w = 0$$

While for firm 2 we can say:

$$\max \pi_2 = P_2 f_2(y_2, x_1) - w y_2 + P_1 f_1(y_1)$$

$$\partial \pi_2 / \partial y_2 = P_2 \partial f_2/\partial y_2 - w = 0;$$

$$\partial \pi_2 / \partial x_1 = P_2 \partial f_2/\partial x_1 + t P_1 = 0$$

by substituting we obtain:

$$t = \frac{P_2 \partial f_2 / \partial x_1}{P_2 \partial f_2 / \partial x_1 - w / df_1 / dy_1} ;$$

The sign of t will depend on whether the generated externality is positive or negative. In the case it is positive (negative) t is positive (negative). It is negative if it represents a tax for firm 1 and positive if it represents a grant for firm 1.

This statement yields t^*, the optimum tax, where $1 > t^* > 0$ is positive for the negative external effect (since both numerator and denominator are negative) and lower than unit as denominator is higher in absolute value than numerator.

Application of this taxing solution is not easy since it requires some information from the government which is difficult to obtain.

5.6.2   Negotiation and Election Problems between Agents

The competitive model ignores non-convexities, especially the existence of firms with increasing returns. The assumption of convexity in consumers' preferences as well as in production sets is justified from the "decreasing marginal utility" and "decreasing marginal returns" laws.

The existence of firms with increasing returns leads to natural monopolies in some specific sectors (telecommunications, electricity, banking, railway, etc.), which leads to fixing prices over the marginal costs, thus losing equality between marginal rates of transformation and prices. Due to this, optimality disappears and the market equilibrium is not efficient.

5.6.2.1 Non-Convexities in Preferences

The existence of consumers with non-convex preferences of the type in the following figure provides a consumer's discontinuous demand function. In view of discontinuous demand functions it is easy to give examples where no perfect competition equilibrium exists.

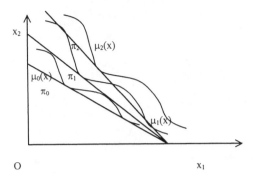

Fig. 5.22

5.6.2.2 Non-Convexities and General Equilibrium

We must question whether non-convexities continue being so important with respect to production and consumption simultaneously. In fact they are. In order to illustrate this answer observe the following figure:

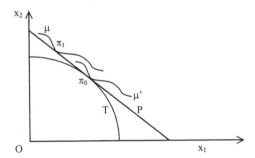

Fig. 5.23

In the above figure π_0 is not a Pareto optimum because, with the same prices the consumer prefers to be at combination π_1 with a higher utility.

Another illustration could be the following:

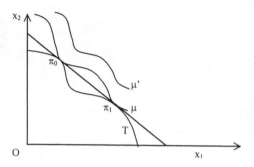

Fig. 5.24

In the above figure there are two possible equilibriums π_0, π_1, equally preferred by consumer and producer. We cannot guarantee the existence of only one competitive general equilibrium. Moreover, not only the existence of convexities is required but also the fact that these convexities must be strict because there may be situations when equilibrium does not exist as in the following figure:

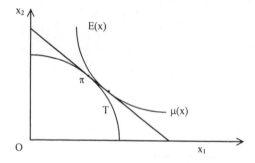

Fig. 5.25

In the above figure the information about prices is insufficient for the producer to be at π. Otherwise we should have information about the quantities provided by the economic activity, for example. Moreover, the strict non-convexity situation can be illustrated for $\mu(x)$ as in the following figure:

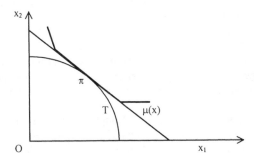

Fig. 5.26

In addition, it may also happen that:

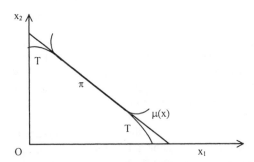

Fig. 5.27

In any of the previous situations, the main advantage of the second Welfare Theorem (we can choose a Pareto optimum which seems desirable and obtain it by means of a decentralized mechanism of prices) is lost.

5.6.3 Information Problems: Universality, Transaction Costs, Asymmetries and Anonymity

5.6.3.1 Universality: The Conventional Theory of the Firm and the Incomplete Contracts

A basic institutional assumption in the competitive general equilibrium model is the Market Universality. That is to say, each good has a market and price. In other words, markets are full or universal and they do not imply any risk either for consumers or for producers. However, things are not usually like this. Agents do not know what will happen next day or in the future economic world. Although agents are logical and try to draw up complete contracts, these contracts do not actually exist since it is impossible to make a whole list of any possible eventuality that may be given in life. Desired markets are those of specific goods and for specific purposes (*qui pro quo*). This would lead to increasingly extensive contracts which would include a never-ending list of eventualities and interpreting these contracts would lead to new costs. The costs derived from drawing up these contracts as well as from guaranteeing their general performance are denominated transaction costs.

In short, in the competitive general equilibrium model we do not mention uncertainty. Our model has a temporal, very mechanical reading because an umbrella today may be a different good tomorrow. When we assume that there are full markets or markets for all goods, we are assuming that there are future markets for all goods, which is impossible except for the period of human slavery.

The conventional theory of the firm – the one in the Economy textbooks - presents the businessman as a profit maximizing agent and the firm as a black box where productive inputs are introduced and final outputs are released. Inputs are hired in competitive markets and outputs are also sold in competitive markets. Such a firm is efficient and enables us to establish the first welfare theorem: with competitive markets the economy reaches an state of efficiency defined in terms of Pareto optimum state.

However, the role played by ownership in the conventional theory of the firm is limited to the distribution of wealth. The ownership of the firm is reflected in its capital; in the goods which produce other goods. In a fully specified competitive general equilibrium model there is not room for an economy of returns (either increasing or decreasing). All the firms must have constant returns to scale and the extraordinary profits will always be zero.

From a partial competitive equilibrium model, the role of ownership is even more limited. The rich are rich and the poor are poor. Moreover, income redistribution does not affect in any way property redistribution in society. The result is the one already shown as the first welfare theorem but it could also be formulated in terms of the Coase Theorem: it does not matter who has the rights over the goods, exchanges will be efficiently carried out.

As there is only one way to make a firm efficient there is only one way to make a society efficient. As remarked, a firm is efficient when it works with full markets. This fictitious firm signs contracts in every market fully specifying every outcome. There is no unexpected accident or eventuality which has not been foreseen at the initial time (zero time or contract signing time). Once all contracts have been signed it is very difficult to distinguish between what happens inside or outside the firm. Everything happens according to an optimization program to which shadow prices are allocated in such a way that these prices exactly coincide with the prices established in competitive markets.

This approach of the firm in the conventional theory or in the general equilibrium model (Walras-Arrow-Debreu) is limited. A broader and more realistic theory of the firm is required where market universality fails. Such a broader theory can be provided by two procedures.

i) By introducing the idea of transaction costs.
ii) By introducing the idea of information asymmetries.

5.6.3.2 The Theory of the Firm: Transaction Approach

At the late thirties, Coase observed that the conventional theory of the firm did not specified what should be done inside the firm. The firm works independently and the economy functions analogously to the firm. In order to solve this problem, Coase stated that the firms hire inside and outside the firm, thus incurring in different transaction costs.

This approach of the theory of transaction cost later developed by Williamson (1985) tells us that it is impossible to draw up a contract which takes into account every possible outcome. On the whole, the theory of the contracts states that there is no use in making contracts more extensive. If contracts are incomplete a role of ownership emerges which did not exist in complete contracts. In some way, we have an operational answer to the question of what is the meaning of ownership. In complete markets ownership is a source of income, the same as other factors of production, but this definition is almost empty, it says very little about the meaning of ownership. However, in incomplete markets, by ownership we mean the control rights remaining once the contract has been specified, in other words, the right to make the first proposal or the right to negotiate from the dominating position. Ownership is the right to do whatever one wants – provided it is not prohibited by law – once the contracts have been signed.

Grossman and Hart (1986) support the idea that ownership means the control rights remaining once the contract has been specified. In other words, it means the control of the residual rights.

5.6.3.3 The Theory of the Firm: Information Asymmetries Approach

Classic examples of asymmetries in information are those characteristic of the problem of principal and agent in their varieties of moral risk, adverse selection as well as signaling and self-selection.

Hayeck highly focused on the new theory of the firm with asymmetric information while Coase stressed the new theory based upon transaction costs.

In order to give an illustrative interpretation of Hayeck, Hart showed the problem of asymmetric information in bilateral terms: with two agents we can represent, in terms of asymmetric information, the same as with all the individuals of market. With stylized versions we can develop a theory of the firm using the asymmetric information approach, which will allow us to find an ownership structure with higher possibilities to obtain an efficient result.

Such stylized model could be the following. There are two contract parties: A and B; two time periods: 1 and 2 and a technology which depends on the inputs provided by A and B in time period 2. Graphically:

OUTPUT

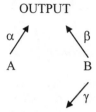

$\alpha = (1, 0); c_\alpha (0) = 0; c_\alpha (1) = 1$
$\beta = (1, 0); c_\beta (0) = 0; c_\beta (1) = 1$
$\gamma = (1, 0); c_\gamma (0) = 0; c_\gamma (1) = 1$

Where the production function is:

$$F (\alpha, \beta, \gamma) = 3\gamma (\alpha + \beta)$$

And where γ is the investment which must be done by B in period 1 in order to guarantee inputs (β) in period 2. If there are incentives individual B will invest in the first period, otherwise, he will not do so. The structure of the problem must make it possible that the profits obtained from the investment of γ are for B, the individual who invests or makes effort. The ideal contract between A and B would be that in which everything were observable.

If contracting in period 1 were possible contracts on input deliveries could be done in period 2. This is a new situation of complete markets. In this case there could be two ownership structures. In the first one, the owner is A while in the second one the owner is B. In this procedure, one proposes himself to be the owner and the other one agrees as the contracting parties will share the surplus. In other words:

Owner A
$F (\alpha, \beta, \gamma) = 3(1) [1+1] = 6 = $ Returns
$C_\alpha (1) + C_\beta (1) + C_\gamma (1) = 3 = $ Costs
$6 - 3 = $ Surplus

Being A the owner, surplus would be of 3 units and B would bear a cost of $C_\beta (1)$ $+ C_\gamma (1) = 2$ units, therefore B would surely produce in the second period if he is supplied with $2+\varepsilon$. Since A gets $3-(2+\varepsilon)$, he always has a guaranteed margin for production.

Alternatively, being B the owner:

Owner B
$F (\alpha, \beta, \gamma) = 3(1) [1+1] = 6 = $ Returns
$C_\alpha (1) + C_\beta (1) + C_\gamma (1) = 3 = $ Costs
$6 - 2 = $ Surplus

In this case, the surplus of B is 3 units and A bears a cost of $C_\alpha (1) = 1$ units, then A will surely produce in the second period if B is supplied with 1+ε. As B gets 3+(1+ε) he is always guaranteed a margin for production.

There is optimality and a positive profit in both cases so the ownership structure does not affect efficiency. This result again reminds us of the Coase theorem above-formulated in the transaction costs.

We will now expose the above model under a transaction cost approach. Assume that a contract cannot be signed in period 1 for period 2 because there is uncertainty. Moreover, assume that there is not asymmetric information, in other words, that both players have the same information. As in the case of the above model, either A or B may be the owner. Let's remember that in the information asymmetry model ownership implied a surplus of 3 units, in other words:

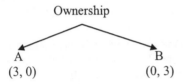

Ownership

A
(3, 0)

B
(0, 3)

In the present model there is uncertainty. During period 1 B may have invested and owns one unit of γ, or he may not have invested.

Assume that A is the owner. Note that being the owner implies being the one who makes proposals. Also assume that individual B has invested one unit of γ and that A suggests B provide him with one unit of β. Therefore:

Owner A

$F (\alpha, \beta, \gamma) = 3(1) [1+1] = 6 = $ Returns
$C_\alpha (1) + C_\beta (1) = 2 = $ Costs
$6 - 2 = $ Surplus

Individual A will have a surplus of 4 units while individual B will bear a cost of $C_\gamma (1) = 1$, one unit of γ, therefore the result is (4, -1). As B made his productive investment in period 1 he cannot retreat in period 2 since A will not allow him to.

If individual B, rather than A, were the owner, then he could propose A to provide him with one unit of α. Therefore:

Owner B

$F (\alpha, \beta, \gamma) = 3(1) [1+1] = 6 = $ Returns
$C_\alpha (1) + C_\beta (1) + C_\gamma (1) = 3 = $ Costs
$6 - 3 = $ Surplus

Individual B will have a surplus of 3 units and individual A will have a cost of zero units. Then, the result will be (0, 3).

In conclusion, the results, depending on the owner, are (4, -1) or (0, 3), in other words:

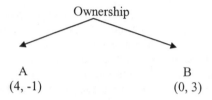

Ownership

A
(4, -1)

B
(0, 3)

If A is the owner, agent B will not invest γ as A may expropriate him his investment. However, if B is the owner, that is to say, the individual who invests γ, then production is guaranteed.

With incomplete markets, if A is the owner we will have under-investment in productive resources by non-owner agent B. If those who invest are owners – the ones with capacity of making proposals –, then there will be efficient production. In the conventional theory of the firm, agents A and B are at equal positions in the productive process. In the transaction cost approach agent B controls A.

From this application of the contract theory some conclusions may be reached on the optimum structure of the firm as regards who must provide the inputs (α, β, γ) of the firm.

Investment generates innovation so the existence of innovation requires investment, so we must say that, for innovation to exist the profits must be received only by those who have invested.

By extending the above model towards a bigger symmetry, we may represent the following:

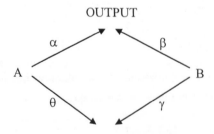

OUTPUT

α   β

A   B

θ   γ

Where the production function is:

$$F(\alpha, \beta, \gamma, \theta) = (\theta + \gamma)(\alpha + \beta)$$

In this case, the efficient procedure continues being the contribution of the two agents in such a way that the following results are obtained and they may be represented as:

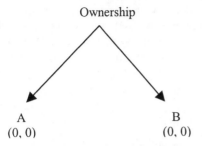

Ownership

A   B
(0, 0)   (0, 0)

This is a competitive result in which the Walras-Debreu model operates. However, nothing guarantees that this result is obtained.

If individual A is the owner (the one who makes proposals), he will expropriate B and the result will be:

Owner A ⟶ Result (1, -1)

If, on the contrary, B is the owner, we will have that:

Owner B ⟶ Result (-1, 1)

If we consider the fact of being the owner as a lottery with a probability of 50:50 between individuals A and B, we could attain the competitive result.

5.6.3.3.1 Problem of Moral Risk (1)

In theory, the manager of a firm follows the suggestions of the owner of such firm. The manager is an agent with his own interests and the consequences of his actions are not directly observable. Divergence between the interests of the owner or owners of the firm and the manager's interests may not be big because when the manager maximizes the profits of the firm he manages, he gains confidence and generally has a share in said profits. The market is a final discipline: if the firm operates badly, it will have to shut down. However, the manager's interests may be very different from the owners' and in such cases, one should expect a judicial system which could adequately condemn these cases. Usually, the judicial system is not capable of solving these problems and, in order to impose disciplinary actions, it usually establishes contracts between principal and agent.
Besides, if the principal is not a single one, controlling of the agent by the principal (shareholders) becomes a public good. On the other hand, some shareholders may realize that they can act as *free-riders* of the other shareholders who make an effort to control de managers.

5.6.3.3.2 Problem of Adverse Selection (2)

Two cases of adverse selection which are widely known in the economic literature will be exposed here. In the first case the Akerlof model (1970) will be briefly described for the quality of cars. The second case refers to a labor market. In this case productivities are known by workers and there is an unknown quantity for the firm.

The Akerlof model (1970) can be illustrated with a simple example. Assume a market of 200 used cars of which 100 are bargains and 100 are old crocks. Also assume that the buyer lacks the information necessary to distinguish the bargain from the old crock but he is sure he would pay 100 m.u. for a bargain while he would pay 50 m.u. for an old crock. If there is a 50% possibility of a car being either a bargain or an old crock, the buyer would be willing to pay:

½ (100/100) 100 + ½ (100/100) 50 = 75 m.u.

However, with 75 m.u. he would only get an old crock. At this price there would only be old crocks in the market and there would be no exchanges. In order to solve this problem, bargain car sellers must give a sign that they are offering a good car rather than an old crock. Such a sign could be offering a guarantee period to reassure buyers.

In the case of the labor market we will assume that there are as many firms as consumers. Firms have constant returns to scale and workers are indicated by a parameter with uniform productivity distribution α, where α indicates 1 hour of productivity and this may vary between $(\underline{\alpha}, \overline{\alpha})$,

$\underline{\alpha}$ $\overline{\alpha}$

being $\overline{\alpha}$ one hour of quality work, which is equivalent to several hours of normal work $\underline{\alpha}$.

Assuming a reserve value r, which indicates a second technology which allows us to transform labor units into r consumption units, notwithstanding quality, and assuming also perfect visibility such that it is possible to observe each level of work quality, for example from each produced good, then, each level of work will be offered to a different firm. There will be continuous set of firms where each firm makes null profits for a distinct wage and this will be the optimum result.

In other words, the optimum result will coincide with the Walras solution and workers will be employed for all the different productivities. As we denominate r reserve value of labor units, we will have that:

With $\alpha < r \Rightarrow$ workers are employed outside the system

With $\alpha \geq r \Rightarrow$ workers are employed within the system with wage $w(\alpha) \geq r$

Assume now that there is not perfect information. In the above case α is not observable, therefore, we will have a single market and a single price rather than continuous set of markets. In this situation, we will have a tentative wage w and there will be two cases:

- That $w \geq r$, where the labor supply equals all the workers with productivities within interval $[\underline{\alpha}, \overline{\alpha}]$; in other words, the mean productivity is: MeP = $(\underline{\alpha} + \overline{\alpha})/2$.

- That $w < r$, where the labor supply is null.

If the mean productivity equals wage, that is to say, if

$$w = MeP = (\underline{\alpha} + \overline{\alpha})/2$$

then, there will be equilibrium.
 Graphically:

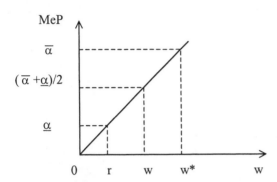

Fig. 5.28

In other words, highly-skilled workers, who would receive a wage w*, become disadvantaged and unskilled workers earn more, receiving a wage r.
 The market is closed with a non-optimum result. In order to solve this problem, we will allow the worker to give a sign of his capacity. This sign may be a university degree. Assume that workers have utility functions of the type:

$$U = U (w, e)$$

such that the indifference curves of highly-skilled workers are flatter than those of unskilled workers, which implies that:

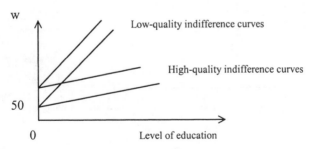

Fig. 5.29

The reason for this is that university studies require more effort from those individuals with less capacity.

The wage by levels of education may be constant such as in the following figure:

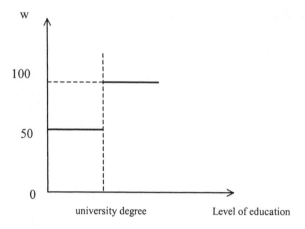

Fig. 5.30

Now, by superposing the two above figures:

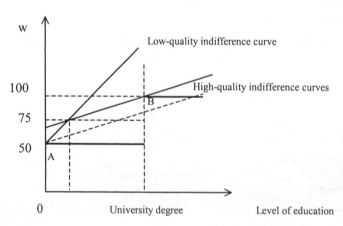

Fig. 5.31

If education acts as a sign, unskilled workers receive a wage of 50 and highly-skilled workers receive a wage of 100. Everything would be apparently solved. However, assume now that the cost of studying at the university and getting the degree is higher than the 25 m.u. earned by the highly-skilled worker. In this case, the situation of this highly-skilled or highly-productive worker becomes worse and therefore, the total surplus of market decreases by the quantity of the cost of education as a consequence of the sign. If finally, all the workers earn the same notwithstanding their education, then, education represents a social cost which does not provide social benefits. This is a paradoxical conclusion which cannot be considered as a statement. What information asymmetries actually mean is that an economy at a specific time can have too much education since this is used as a sign which produces higher returns in comparison with those with those obtained when there is lower education.

5.6.3.3.3 Signaling and Self-selection (3)

This section presents two models: the traditional sign-transmission model, attributed to Spence (1974) and the self-selection model of Rothschidd and Stiglitz (1996).

In Spence's model firms act in a perfect competition market with constant returns to scale, where e is the level of education, which is considered as non-productive but which has a cost for those workers who get it.

On the other hand, there are two types of workers: highly-skilled or unskilled workers.

If such skills were observable the levels of education would provide the equilibriums as in the following figure:

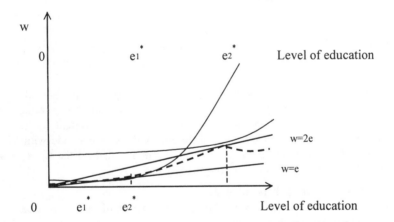

Fig. 5.32

Workers of the two types can be observed and we reach a separating equilibrium.

For this equilibrium to work, it is required that an anticipated-wages function w(e) exists, which will enable workers to know in advance that they will be paid depending on their education e. On the other hand a likelihood distribution qᵢ must exist over the set of levels of education for each type of worker, which indicates or shows the proportion of workers of type t who choose the level of education e in equilibrium. In other words, it must be true that:

i) For each type of worker and level of education e, $q_t > 0$, only if $U_t[w(e), e]$ reaches the maximum value for some level of education. In other words, workers choose the level of education which maximizes their utility. In short, they carry out self-selection.

ii) For each level of education such that $q_1(e) + q_2(e) > 0$ the wage equals the addition of the conditioned likelihood that workers are unskilled or highly-skilled according to the Bayes Law.

$$w(e) = \frac{0,5q_1(e)}{0,5q_1(e) + 0,5q_2(e)} \, e + \frac{0,5q_2(e)}{0,5q_1(e) + 0,5q_2(e)} \, 2e$$

Where w(e) is the conditioned expected wage value of a worker with education e and, due to competition between the firms, the wage tends to be such wage value.

Assuming that firms are neutral to the risk and making:

$$\frac{0,5q_1(e)}{0,5q_1(e) + 0,5q_2(e)} = \theta(e)$$

we have:

$$w(e) = \theta(e)\, e + [1 - \theta(e)]\, 2e$$

then:

$$w(e) = \theta(e)\, e - 2e - \theta(e)\, 2e = 2e - \theta(e)\, e;$$

$$w(e) = e\, [e - \theta(e)]$$

Where function w(e) indicates the hypotheses made by workers about the wages they will receive depending on the level of education they choose, in other words, that whish is represented in the above figure with a discontinuous line. This function must always be below the indifference curves or coincide with them at the points of the level of education chosen. Assuming that all the workers make the same hypotheses, function w(e) may satisfy that:

i)   It is non-negative as there is not slavery.
ii) It must take values within interval [e, 2e], in other words, $e \le w(e) \le 2e$.
iii) w(e)/e must be non-decreasing.

In the above figure ii) and iii) properties are not satisfied, however, in the figure below these properties are satisfied and unskilled workers choose e_1 which is their optimum.

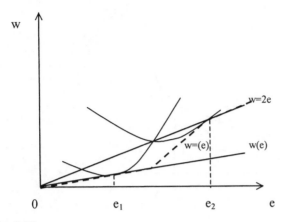

Fig. 5.33

If all the workers are grouped into a single level of education (e*), the new equilibrium is denominated grouping equilibrium. Assuming that the number of highly-skilled workers is the same as that of unskilled workers, the likelihood of being unskilled and choosing e* is $\alpha(e*) = 0.5$ and the wages offered are:

$$w(e*) = e* [2 - \alpha(e)] = e* (2 - 0.5) = 1.5 \, e$$

In order to represent it graphically, function $w(e)$ must be curved at point e*, thus, it will be tangent to the indifferent curves at said point e* and will go below them.

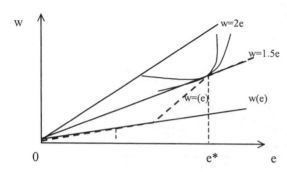

Fig. 5.34

In the Rothschidd and Stiglitz model (1996) workers apply the self-selection condition from the different contracts that exist. In this case, the firms are the ones which anticipate and offer a menu of contracts to workers and, according to this offer, the workers choose the education they wish.

The model assumptions are the following:

i) There is a selection rule for workers under which they are allocated the different contracts. In other words, each category of worker has a possibility of distribution q_t, which must satisfy the following:

   a) $q_t > 0$, if the worker maximizes his utility. In other words, each worker is assigned the best contract for him: his optimum.

   b) Provided that $q_1 + q_2 > 0$, the firms offer contracts if:

$$w \le \frac{0{,}5q_1}{0{,}5q_1 + 0{,}5q_2} e + \frac{0{,}5q_2}{0{,}5q_1 + 0{,}5q_2} 2e$$

   w being the wage and the second member of the inequality being the conditioned expected value of a worker with a level of education e.

ii) A menu of contracts $\{(w^1, e^1), (w^2, e^2), ..., (w^n, e^n)\}$.

iii) There cannot be any additional contract to the menu which offers positive profits to the firm.

With these assumptions, let's see how the model works from the following figure:

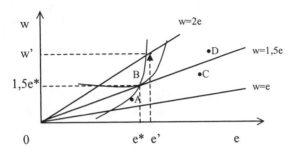

Fig. 5.35

The menu of contracts offered by the firm are the gross points A, B, C and D. The best one for both types of workers is point B, level of education e* and wage 1.5e* since, with this contract, the highest level of utility is reached. However, if a firm offers the contract which corresponds to e' and w' it will attract highly-skilled workers (thus having a higher level of utility) while it will not attract unskilled workers so the firm will obtain profits and no equilibrium will exist.

In equilibrium, it is impossible for a contract to be agreed by both types of workers at the same time and the only equilibriums, according to this model, will be separating equlibriums.

5.6.4 Anonymity

There are other cases of transactions between small groups of agents. In such cases the agents can be identified and anonymity is lost. In these situations the appeal of the second welfare theorem is again lost because it is very difficult to manage *lumpsum tax* transferences. For this to happen, it should be possible to observe the agents' returns and that such agents (being a few and observed) do not develop strategic behaviors.

Moreover, although the economic authority could have all the information to develop *lumpsum tax* transferences this transference system should be inevitable.

In short, the second welfare theorem has important deficiencies that prevent it from being operative.

Bibliographic References

Akerlof, G.: The Market for Lemons: Quality Uncertainty and the Market Mechanism. Quarterly Journal of Economics 89, 488-500 (1970)

Arrow, K. J.: Social Choice and Individual Values. New York: John Wiley & Sons 1951

Bergson, A.: A reformulation of certain aspects of welfare economics. Quarterly Journal of Economics 52, 31-34 (1938)

Coase, R.: The problem of Social Cost. Journal of law and economics, 1-44 (1960)

Grosman, S. J., Hart, O. D.: An analysis of the principal-agent problem. Econometrica 51, 7-45 (1983)

Laffont, J. J.: Fundamentals of public Economics. Cambridge, Mass.: MIT Press 1988

Lancaster, K., Lipsey, R. G.: The General Theory of Second Best. Review of Economics Studies 24, 11-32 (1956)

Morgensten, O., von Newman, J.: Theory of games and Economic Behavior. Princeton: Princeton University Press 1944

Pigou, A. C.: The Economics of Welfare. London: MacMillan 1932

Rothschild, M., Stiglitz: Equilibrium in competitive insurance markets: an essay in the economics of imperfect information. Quarterly Economic Journal of Economics 80, 629-649 (1976)

Spence, A. M.: Market Signaling. Cambridge, Mass.: Harvard University Press 1974

Sen, A.: Individual Choice and Social Welfare. San Francisco: Holden Day 1970

Sen, A. K.: On Weight and Measures: Informational Constraints in Social Welfare Analysis. Econometrica 45, 1539-72 (1977)

Sen, A.: Social Choice Theory. Chap 22 in: Handbook of Mathemathical Economics. K. Arrow, M. Intriligator ed. Amsterdam: North-Holland 1986

Span, R. M.: Collective Consumption of Private Goods. Public Choice 20, 63-81 (1974)

Spulber, D. F.: Regulation and markets. Cambridge, Mass.: MIT Press 1989

Stigler, G. J.: General Economic Conditions and Natural Elections. American Economic Review 63, 160-7 (1973)

Williamson, O.: The Economic Institution of capitalism. New York: Free Press 1985

6 Social Choice and Individual Freedom: A Thematic Guide

6.1 Market Failures and Government Failures

We have seen that for every "market" failure there is a correcting action which hypothetically solves the problem.

Are these corrections actually possible?

They are hardly ever

Why? Due to three types of causes or problems which will be exposed below in 6.1.1, 6.1.2 and 6.1.3.

6.1.1 The Government's Problems in Property Rights Allocation

The government faces problems of property rights allocation: it does not properly identify either external cost/benefits or the individual demands for public goods.

6.1.2 Information Problems

The government faces information problems and maybe the most important is the agency problem or principal-agent relationship because of which government agents do not act properly. This does not mean that there exist prejudices against burocrats, we only recognize that when one delegates responsibilities there is always inefficiency. The representative's objectives do not always coincide with the principal's and, after all, although the political representative and the bureaucrat basically represent the citizens, they search for their own goals.

The representative's problem also exists in private firms (employer as compared with employee), in mercantile societies (manager as compared with partners) and in joint-stock companies (president of the Administrative Board as compared with shareholders). Such problem has led to deontological actions as the Cadlbury Report, which tries to suggest ethical behaviors more in accordance with the shareholders' interests.

6.1.3 The Government's Problems in Negotiation and Choice

In the social choice theory, the key problem is how to define social preferences: how is it possible to know whether the choice of building a library is better or worse than building a swimming-pool? How can we change from individual to collective preferences? Is voting enough? Have individuals enough incentives to vote? What happens when individuals vote for a particular political party and this party forms a coalition with other parties? How do bureaucrats behave in government? What is the best voting system if different answers can be provided to the same popular concern by the different systems? Can the government expand indefinitely? What is role of the pressure groups?

The government faces negotiation and choice problems: the voting market is not efficient. It is not sufficient to punish the politician or the bureaucrat by voting another politician or party which supports other bureaucrats or less bureaucracy. The political market is inefficient because it presents numerous problems, which will be exposed below: 6.1.3.1 to 6.1.3.9.

6.1.3.1 The Voting Order Paradox

Assuming we have three individuals who must choose one of these three alternatives: A, B and C. The following table shows the order of preferences of each individual:

		1st choice	2nd choice	3rd choice
Individual	1	A	B	C
Individual	2	B	C	A
Individual	3	C	A	B

With this situation we will proceed to submit choice A and B to a vote. In this case, choice A has 2 votes against choice B which has 1 as individuals 1 and 3 vote for A and individual 2 votes for B. If B and C are submitted to a vote, B has 2 votes against C which has 1 as individuals 1 and 2 vote for B and individual 3 votes for C. If A and C are now submitted to a vote, C has 2 votes against A which has 1 vote as individuals 2 and 3 vote for C and individual 1 votes for A.

In other words, the so generated social preference order turns out to be intransitive.

6.1.3.2 Impossibility of Aggregation of Personal Preferences

The Arrow Theorem of Impossibility:

Given a mechanism to change from individual to social preferences, the resulting social preference order may always be either incomplete or intransitive, except for the case in which the social preference order is defined as coincident with that of a particular individual (the dictator) with "normal" preferences, in other words, with complete and transitive preferences.

Therefore, no ideal voting rule nor ideal constitution exist. In short, there is no voting rule which "a priori" may not be susceptible to manipulation by someone and which guarantees consistent results.

Arrow's result is worrying. Arrow, in his doctoral thesis, "Social Choice and Individual Values" (1951), posed questions such as: How can we know which are the preferences of society when it is the individual preferences that we know? Is there any social decision rule par excellence? In his attempt to find answers to these questions, he proposed a rule for the aggregation of individual preferences in social orderings which should satisfy four conditions. Arrow's brilliant result, known as the General Theorem of Impossibility, states that there is no social welfare function which satisfies the four conditions. We will now examine the four conditions.

The first condition states that the social choice from a subset of choices must only depend on the individuals' ordering of these choices rather than on their preferences in relation with different "irrelevant" alternatives which do not intervene in the election. This is Condition I of Independence from Irrelevant Alternatives.

The second condition states that the social welfare function (SWF) must include all the logically possible combinations of individual ordering. The ideal constitution must be for every set of individuals, whatever their preferences may be. This is Condition II of Restricted Domain.

The third condition states that the SWF must respect the Pareto criterion: if all the individuals strictly prefer situation α to β, then, the SWF must be such that α be socially preferred to β. This is Condition P of the Pareto Criterion.

The fourth condition states that there must not be any dictator. That is to say, no individual must exist such that whenever he/she prefers α to β, all the society must also prefer α to β. This is Condition D of Dictatorship Inexistence.

Therefore, the Arrow General Theorem of Impossibility can be expressed by stating that there is no collective decision rule which guarantees satisfaction of the four Arrow's conditions in all places at all times, or that the only rule which guarantees the first three in every possible situation is the dictatorship. Sean (1977) presents the development of the theory of social choice, in which the logical implications of the four conditions are analyzed in detail.

6.1.3.3 Problems in the Majority, Simple and Proportional Choice Systems

Simple majority or qualified majority, majority or proportional system, unanimity..., are choice rules adopted depending on the social choice to decide the existence of so large a variety of rules. These rules are an example of the imperfection of choice systems themselves. If there were a better system it would probably be a single one.

6.1.3.4 The Average Voter Paradox

Hotelling presented in 1929 the average voter theorem as a result of the representative two-party democracy (Müeller, 1979). Assuming that voters have the possibility to choose different political parties from the left and the right within a linear spectrum thus:

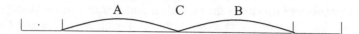

It is assumed that a voter prefers a party which adopts a particular standing, for instance, A, B and C. The farther the political party is from this standing preferred by the voter, the less desirable it will be. If individuals' preferences are uniformly distributed along ACB, then, both parties, A and B will have incentives to offer political programs similar to those of the center with the aim of increasing their votes so that, all the parties will finally struggle for the center.

According to Olson (1965, 1982) two conditions must be satisfied for a collective action to be produced. The first condition is that the group of individuals who may benefit from the collective action is sufficiently small. The second condition is that "selective incentives" exist, in other words, individualized prizes or penalizations which encourage people to get involved in the collective action. For instance, a professional association usually charge rates to its affiliates, who in turn receive not only defense of their professional interests but also other collateral benefits such as soft loans, housing associations, etc.

Satisfying only one of the two Olson conditions, there are already clear reasons to expect that a collective action will be produced.

However, we will mention below some cases where Olson conditions do not seem to be sufficient to explain the collective action in 6.2.1, 6.2.2, 6.2.3 and 6.2.4.

6.1.3.5 Key Parties and Political Coalitions

The existence of key parties and coalitions for governing can lead to instability cycles, turncoats, etc.

6.1.3.6 The Maximizing Bureaucrat Paradox

The lack of incentives makes bureaucrats inefficient. The bureaucrat generally maximizes budgets. Introducing competition among bureaucratic agencies may contribute to solve problems but it is not likely.

6.1.3.7 The Non-Representative Democracy Paradox

Direct or non-representative democracy, for example, through Internet, may present problems because citizens may not have incentives, the time or the knowledge necessary to improve their direct involvement in the process in comparison with representative democracy.

6.1.3.8 The Taxes Paradox

Tax restrictions to the Leviathan of the government, which maximizes budget and expenditure. Broad tax bases asphyxiate citizens. The aim is to maximize the recommended income by means of optimum taxes. Laffer's curve indicates that, if taxes continue increasing when the tax rate is quite high, tax revenue may finally decrease.

Graphically

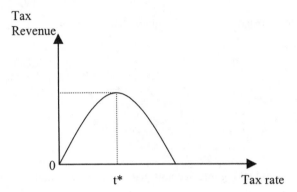

Fig. 6.1

In order to prove this, Laffer made the following labor market model (Varian, 1987):

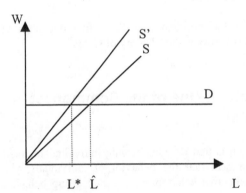

Fig. 6.2

The equilibrium in the labor market will be in ($\hat{W}$, $\hat{L}$). If we now establish a tax rate t to labor and the firm pays wage $\hat{W}$, the worker will receive now W = (1-t) $\hat{W}$. For this reason, the supply will go to the left and become S', so the amount of work will change from $\hat{L}$ to L*.

The tax revenue will be now:

$$I = t\, s(w)\hat{w}$$

where w = (1-t) $\hat{w}$ and s(w) is the labor supply.

The tax revenue variation will be:

$$\frac{dI}{dt} = \left[-t \frac{ds(w)}{dw} \hat{w} + s(w) \right] \hat{w} \ (I)$$

For this expression to be negative, it must be given that:

$$-t \frac{ds(w)}{dw} \hat{w} + s(w) < 0$$

in other words:

$$t \frac{ds(w)}{dw} \hat{w} < s(w)$$

dividing by t s(w):

$$\frac{ds(w)}{dw} \frac{\hat{w}}{s(w)} > \frac{1}{t}$$

multiplying all by (1-t) and taking into account that $w = (1-t) \hat{w}$, then

$$\frac{ds}{dw} \frac{w}{s} > \frac{1-t}{t}$$

Observe that the first member of this expression is the labor supply elasticity. Therefore, we can conclude that Laffer's effect - i.e; the increase of tax rate reduces tax revenue - will occur only if labor supply elasticity is higher than (1-t)/t.

6.1.3.9 The Theory of Pressure Groups

The power of pressure groups on the political and legislative decisions is sometimes excessive. A variety of this theory is the "Theory of Clubs".

6.2
Problems of Collective Action: One of the Commonest Collective Actions is Voting

The first problem of collective action is that of transforming individual interests into collective interests. We can expect that the behavior of individuals with similar interests may generate a collective behavior or a social group behavior which is coherent with those similar interests. For instance: professional associations, sports clubs, trade unions, etc. constitute groups with similar interests and we can expect that their behaviors are governed by the utility maximization principle.

The second problem of collective action is the "free rider" problem. Carrying out a collective action always means some costs for those individuals who are involved in it. However, the collective action finally provides a public good. This means that we are facing the problem of the private provision of public goods.

The third problem is in fact previous to the collective action, it consists of adequately defining the group's interest. We are really stating that there is a social election problem previous to the collective action problems.

6.2.1 The Voting Paradox

At first, every voter would wonder what's the reason of voting if one vote is decisive only in the case of draw? What is the likelihood of a single vote being decisive? This is the Voting Paradox.

6.2.2 Strategic Voting

The strategic vote is simply a deliberate vote, that is to say, a vote with a view to obtaining a result. The voter is interested in hiding his/her true preferences with the aim of getting the desired result. There are at least two important facts in strategic voting. The first is the fact that the existence of strategic voting "affects" the collective decision processes. This means that nothing guarantees that the strategic votes neutralize one another. The second is that there is no voting system which may be considered invulnerable to any type of strategy.

6.2.3 The Revolution Paradox and the Theory of the Coup d'Etat

Another widely known paradox is that relative to the revolution. When the vote does not represent the popular feeling or that of the voter, there a choice of a revolution. Being involved or not in the possible revolution will provide either benefits or losses. If the revolution is sucessful the rebel may aspire to a position in the new regime. However, if revolution fails the rebel may go to prison or even be executed and the likelihood of sucess estimated by the citizen is close to zero, therefore, a revolution should not be attempted. This is the paradox of revolution. In fact, this theory of revolution explains "the coup d'etat" better than a revolution of many citizens; that is to say, a smaller number of actors who, despite their few probabilities of success, have great potential benefits. This is why coup d'etats are commoner than spontaneous revolutions.

Anyway, we must highlight that citizens are always subjected to the danger of being tyrannized or exploited by a minority or a majority of their fellow citizens so, in such situations they would use their vote to change the political organization or alternatively opt for migration or revolution.

6.2.4 The Migration Paradox

The aspect of migration has been mentioned in above section because the way of action is "voting with their feet". However, if all the individuals did this there would be either an unstable process in which every community would constantly change its offer of public goods and citizens would be constantly emigrating, or, alternatively, an equilibrium situation would be produced where all the communities would offer the same so there would not be any reason for migration. This is the Migration Paradox.

6.3
From the Anarchy and Equilibrium of the "Natural State" to the Constitutional Democracy

Primitive situations of the minimally organized individual or in his "natural state" as well as the change from nomad life to sedentary life lead to the first co-operative solutions. From successive or repeated confrontations between tribes or individuals, from the prisoner's dilemma emerges co-operation and co-operation leads to leadership societies. In fact, authority arises with the evolution of civilization and from this evolution view emerges the state [the sovereign, the constitution and democracy as the least imperfect form of government]. In the 18th century, the French supported with their mercantilist ideas the central role of the State in the economy. As a response to this idea in 1776, Adam Smith published "The wealth of nations". Smith opposed to that idea and stood for the assumption that the invisible hand of the market achieves the best situation for the society.

6.3.1 The Invisible Hand and the Minimal State

In the 18th century, John Stuart Mill and Nassau Seniour promulgated the doctrine "Laissez-faire, laissez-passer". Under this doctrine, the role of the State was reduced to the minimum. Market competition was the best way to defend the rights of society. However, we must say that these classic ideas did not convince everyone. Thus, other 19th century thinkers such as Karl Marx, Sismondi and Robert Owen developed different theories which attributed social problems to private property of capital or production means. For Owen, forming smaller States of people makes population co-operate and be able to solve social problems.
But, what's the meaning of the State?

6.3.2 The State and its Institutions

The State is made up by all the citizens, then, we all are the State. The state organs are something different: The Parliament and the Senate for the central government and, since most western countries have decentralized structures, there are autonomous, provincial and local governments.

In U.S.A. the central government is responsible for national defence, money issue and regulation of inter-regional and international trade. However, the state and municipal governments are responsible for the services of education, police, fire authority, social assistance, libraries, sewage and rubbish collection.

Moreover, in some cases the government decides to nationalize some companies for varied reasons; because it may be a way to control a natural monopoly or because it may provide goods and services for public interests.

6.3.3 The State Origins

Which is the origin of the State? In order to answer this question the following explicative theories are exposed in 6.3.3.1 and 6.3.3.2.

6.3.3.1 Contractual Theories

One of the meanings of State is that of the voluntary union of individuals with a common interest, who sign a "contract" to assign not only certain rights and powers to the State but also duties and obligations to supply certain goods and services whose private provision would not be possible or would result very expensive.

6.3.3.1.1 Rousseau and the Social Contract

The contractual theory of the State is owed to the French philosopher Jean-Jaques Rousseau. Unfortunately, Rousseau does not give any relevant criteria to make political decisions although the basic idea is very interesting: co-operation for the supply of public goods. It is necessary to pursue and find relevant criteria to carry out public choices. Rawls proposes individuals to be situated at an equal initial status with an "ignorance veil" in order to judge what is "fair" or what is not, before knowing, or estimating the likelihood of their function in the society. Rawls supports the idea that if all of us started from an equal position, we all would wish to maximize the welfare of individuals in the lowest status without making concessions. For Rawls, the individuals who conform the State act as if they were individuals who meet together in order to play a game of chance. Thus, before starting to play they establish the game rules, in other words, before delivering the cards and each one knows his game and his chances with respect to other players. Economic life is a game of chance in which Nature distributes attributes and social positions at random. This initial distribution is neither fair nor unfair. What is unfair is that society accepts these random results and that they create institutions which perpetuate such results. Justice implies creating institutions which mitigate the differences or unbalances generated at random. This is the notion of justice as impartiality.

6.3.3.1.2 Rawls and Social Justice

For Rawls, the fair social contract must be based on the following two principles:

6.3.3.1.2.1 The Equality Principle

First principle (or the Equality Principle): everyone must have the same rights and the highest freedom compatible with similar freedoms which belong to the rest of people.

6.3.3.1.2.2 The Difference Principle and the Leximin Rule

Second principle (or the Difference Principle): social and economic inequalities must be ordered in such a way that:

i) it can be guaranteed that they will result advantageous for everyone;

ii) all social values (freedom and opportunity, income, wealth and basic dignity) must be equally distributed among all the individuals unless an unequal distribution of some or all of them is advantageous for all.

Such principles will be lexicographically ordered in such a way that the first one always has priority over the second.

From the first principle we infer that as the society undergoes more economic development it will be more willing to pay for some individuals' freedom.

From the second principle, which also follows a lexicographic ordering, we infer that the welfare of the least advantageous individual must be preferably maximized in comparison with the others' welfare, therefore, inequality would only be justified if this individual's welfare improves. This collective choice rule is known as the Leximin Rule, which is an extension of the Maximin Rule, one of John Rawls' key ideas. By analogy, the welfare of the second least advantageous individual welfare will be maximized afterwards, and so on. In order to illustrate this, table 6.1 is presented with two strategies: S_1 and S_2 for two states of the world B and N:

Table 6.1

	B	N
S_1	0	n
S_2	1/n	1

With rewards

$$\begin{bmatrix} 0, & n \\ 1/n & 1 \end{bmatrix}$$

An individual always chooses the option with the maximum minimum reward (maximin) and it will depend on which are the other rewards . If $n < \infty$ and if $p > 0$ (being p the likelihood of obtaining B and therefore, (1-p) is the likelihood to obtain N) the expected result will never be zero, always being higher than 0.

$$\frac{1}{n} > 0$$

This implies that no amount will be ever paid, no matter how small it is, unless its recovery is not guaranteed – no matter how big the likelihood of recovering it may be .

From here, Rawls extends his theory of the political process by stages: the constitution stage, the parliametary stage, the administrative stage and the judicial stage.

At the initial stage, the magna carta or fair constitution is drawn up, and the parliament, the administration and justice are formed at successive stages.

Moreover, the above analysis proves that the choice of the informational framework determines the different rules of collective choice. One of the examples which better illustrates such informational framework is the example of the fallen angel [Sen (1975)].

A society with 2 individuals: A and B; and two alternatives: A1 and A2; may be represented as in table 6.2.

Table 6.2

	A1	A2
Individual A	10	8
Individual B	4	7
Social welfare	14	15

If we consider the addition of utilities we will choose 2 A rather than 1. Being individual A a happy, rich and healthy motorbike driver and B a bad-tempered, poor and unhealthy individual, in the case of alternative 1, individual A is happy with his motorbike in comparison with the bad-tempered pedestrian. In the case of alternative 2, individual A falls onto the ditch, the motorbike gets spoilt and damaged and this individual gets to be in a worse state than individual B, who split his sides laughing. Curiously, alternative 2 is sociably preferred.

6.3.3.2 Utility Theories

Contractual theories did not employ either utility indexes or other analogous concepts but they mentioned levels of wealth in terms of primary goods such as freedom, dignity, opportunities, the income and the wealth that a society must distribute. Other authors such as Harsang and Vickery have tried to use Rawls' concept of impartiality in order to obtain a social welfare function.

6.4
Final Remarks

Buchanan, Tullock and Leibenstein have applied the notion of impartiality to the analysis of collective decision-making.

These works constitute true bridges between philosophy, welfare and public choice.

In fact, here we come across some of the oldest and most difficult problems which any community may face, such as how to rule with fairness and efficiency?

In short, how to make efficiency and equity compatible.

Bibliographic References

Alchian, A.A and Demsetz, H. (1972): Production, Information Costs and Economic Organization. American Economic Review, 62, 777-96.

Arrow, K. J. (1963): Social Choice and Individual Values, New York: John Wiley & Sons, Inc., 1951, ed.

Buchanan, J.M. (1976): A Hallesian Interpretation of the Rawlsian Difference Principle. Kyklos, 29, 5-25.

Mueller, D.C. (1979): Public Choice. Cambridge University Press.

Olson, M. L. (1965): The logic of collective action. Harvard University Press.

Olson, M. L. (1982): The rise and decline of nations. Yale University Press.

Sen, A.K. (1977): On Weight and Measures: Informational Constraints in Social Welfare Analysis. Econometrica, 45, 1539-72.

Span, R.M. (1974): Collective Consumption of Private Goods. Public Choice, 20, 63-81.

Stigler, G.J. (1973): General Economic Conditions and Natural Elections. American Economic Review, 63, 160-7.

Varian, H. (1987): Intermediate Microeconomics. Norton &Norton.

Contributions to Economics